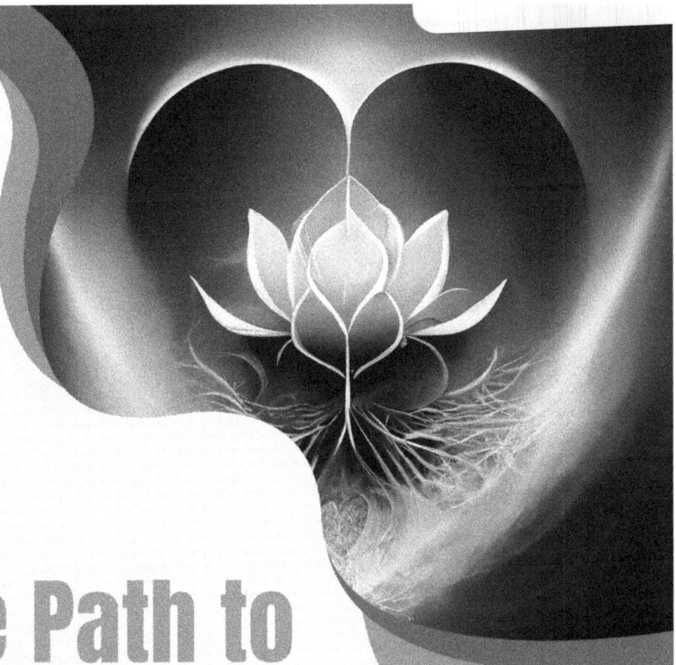

"The Path to Healing

Overcoming Stalking and Harassment"

M L Ruscsak

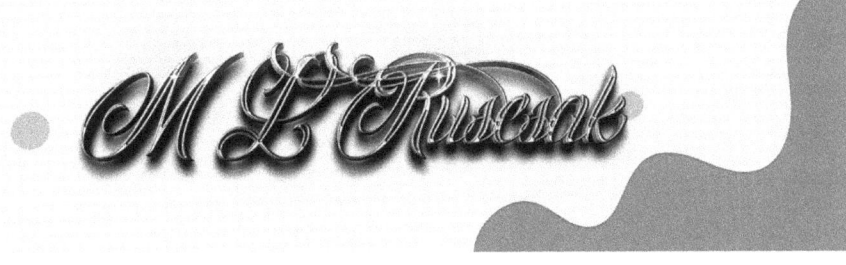

Trient Press
3375 S Rainbow Blvd
#81710, SMB 13135
Las Vegas,NV 89180

Ordering Information:
Quantity sales. Special discounts are available on quantity purchases by corporations, associations, and others. For details, contact the publisher at the address above.
Orders by U.S. trade bookstores and wholesalers. Please contact Trient Press: Tel: (775) 996-3844; or visit www.trientpress.com.

Printed in the United States of America

Publisher's Cataloging-in-Publication data
Ruscsak, M.L.
A title of a book : "The Path to Healing: Overcoming Stalking and Harassment
ISBN
Paperback   979-8-88990-059-7

E-book   979-8-88990-060-3

"The Path to Healing: Overcoming Stalking and Harassment

Table of Contents

Chapter 1 Introduction

Chapter 2 Understanding Stalking and Harassment

Chapter 3 Survivor Stories

Chapter 4 Warning Signs and Prevention

Chapter 5 Coping Strategies

Chapter 6 Legal and Practical Considerations

Chapter 7 Building Resilience and Moving Forward

Chapter 8 Uplifting Quotes

Chapter 9 Conclusion

Chapter 10 Epilogue

INTRODUCTION

I never thought I would be the victim of stalking and harassment. I never thought it could happen to someone like me, someone who had worked hard to build a successful career and a fulfilling life. But it did happen to me, and it shattered my sense of safety and security. It left me feeling violated, scared, and alone.

That's why I'm writing this book, "The Path to Healing: Overcoming Stalking and Harassment." I want to share my story and the stories of other survivors who have gone through similar experiences. I want to shed light on the reality of stalking and harassment, how it can happen to anyone, and how it can affect every aspect of a person's life.

As I sit down to write this book, I am reminded of the immense emotional and mental impact that stalking and harassment can have on a person. The fear, the anxiety, the sense of powerlessness—it can all be overwhelming. It can feel like a heavy weight pressing down on your chest, making it hard to breathe. It can make you doubt yourself, your judgment, and your worth.

But I also know that healing is possible. I know that it takes time, effort, and support, but it is possible. That's why I'm sharing my story, and the stories of other survivors, in this book. I want to offer hope, support, and guidance to those who are going through similar experiences.

It's important to acknowledge the emotional and mental impact of stalking and harassment. It's not just about the physical acts of stalking and harassment—it's about the fear and anxiety that they can create. It's about the sense of violation and betrayal that can come with being targeted by someone you thought you could trust. It's about the sense of powerlessness that can come with not knowing how to protect yourself or your loved ones.

But it's also important to acknowledge that healing is possible. It's possible to move past the fear and the trauma. It's possible to reclaim your sense of safety and security. It's possible to build a life that is free from the shadow of stalking and harassment.

So, in this book, we will explore the different aspects of stalking and harassment, from the warning signs to the legal and practical considerations. We will share survivor stories and uplifting quotes, and we will offer guidance on how to cope, how to heal, and how to move forward.

I want to emphasize that this book is written from a survivor's perspective. I am not a therapist, a lawyer, or an expert in stalking and harassment. I am simply someone who has gone through this experience and who wants to share my story and the stories of others. I hope that this book will offer support, encouragement, and hope to those who are going through similar experiences.

So, let's begin this journey together. Let's explore the path to healing and learn how to overcome stalking and harassment. Let's support each other and build a community of survivors who are strong, resilient, and rising.

Explanation of the book's purpose and the author's perspective

As a survivor of stalking and harassment, I know firsthand how difficult it can be to find the resources and support you need to heal. When I was going through this experience, I felt isolated and alone. I didn't know where to turn or who to talk to. That's why I'm writing this book—to offer support, guidance, and hope to others who are going through similar experiences.

The purpose of this book is to provide a comprehensive guide to overcoming stalking and harassment. We will explore the different aspects of this experience, from understanding what stalking and harassment are to coping strategies, legal considerations, and building resilience. We will share personal stories from survivors, along with uplifting quotes and practical tips.

One of the things that makes this book unique is that it is written from a survivor's perspective. I am not a therapist, a lawyer, or an expert in stalking and harassment. I am simply someone who has gone through this experience and who wants to share what I've learned along the way.

I want to provide a space for survivors to feel seen, heard, and understood. I want to offer a sense of community and support. I want to help survivors reclaim their sense of safety and security and build a life that is free from the shadow of stalking and harassment.

But I also want to be clear that this book is not just for survivors. It's for anyone who wants to learn more about this issue and how to support those who have been affected by it. Stalking and harassment can happen to anyone, and it's important that we all have a better understanding of what it entails.

My hope is that this book will offer a roadmap for healing. It's not a quick fix or an easy solution, but it is possible to move past the fear and trauma. It is possible to reclaim your sense of safety and security. It is possible to build a life that is filled with hope, healing, and rising strong.

Throughout this book, I will share my own experiences, as well as the experiences of other survivors. We will explore the impact of stalking and harassment on mental health and relationships. We will look at warning signs and prevention strategies. We will discuss legal options and practical considerations for staying safe. And we will offer strategies for building resilience and moving forward.

Above all, I want this book to be a message of hope. Healing is possible, and it starts with acknowledging the emotional and mental impact of stalking and harassment. It starts with understanding that you are not alone, and that there is support available. It starts with taking the first step on the path to healing.

Acknowledgement of the emotional and mental impact of stalking and harassment

When it comes to the emotional and mental impact of stalking and harassment, there are no easy answers. It's a complex issue that can leave survivors feeling confused, scared, and overwhelmed.

As a survivor myself, I know firsthand just how deep the emotional scars can run. Stalking and harassment can have a profound impact on your mental health, your relationships, and your sense of safety and security.

One of the most difficult things about this experience is the way it can disrupt your sense of self. When someone is stalking or harassing you, it can feel like they are invading every aspect of your life. You may find yourself constantly looking over your shoulder, questioning your own judgment, and wondering if you're going crazy.

The emotional toll of stalking and harassment can be devastating. It can leave you feeling anxious, depressed, and isolated. It can make it difficult to trust others or feel safe in your own skin. It can lead to a sense of helplessness and hopelessness that can be difficult to shake.

One of the most insidious aspects of this experience is the way it can impact your relationships with others. You may find yourself withdrawing from friends and family, feeling like they don't understand what you're going through. You may feel like you have to put on a brave face and pretend everything is okay, even when it's not. And you may struggle to connect with others in the way you once did, feeling like you're carrying around a secret that you can't share.

It's important to acknowledge the emotional and mental impact of stalking and harassment, both for survivors and for those who want to support them. This is not an easy issue to deal with, and it can be challenging to know how to navigate the emotional fallout.

For survivors, it's important to remember that your feelings are valid. You are not overreacting, and you are not to blame for what has happened to you. It's okay to feel scared, angry, or overwhelmed. It's okay to reach out for help and support.

For those who want to support survivors, it's important to be patient, understanding, and non-judgmental. It's important to listen without trying to offer solutions or advice. And it's important to acknowledge that healing is a process that takes time.

It's also important to remember that healing is possible. While the emotional and mental impact of stalking and harassment can be profound, it is possible to move forward and build a life that is filled with hope and healing. It takes time, patience, and support, but it is possible to reclaim your sense of safety and security.

Throughout this book, we will explore different strategies for coping with the emotional and mental impact of stalking and harassment. We will share personal stories from survivors who have navigated these challenges and come out stronger on the other side. And we will offer practical tips and advice for finding support, building resilience, and moving forward.

It's not an easy journey, but it is possible to rise strong from this experience. It starts with acknowledging the emotional and mental impact of stalking and harassment, and it continues with taking the first steps on the path to healing.

Journal Exercises

Reflect on your journey so far. Take some time to think about your experience with stalking and harassment. What happened?

_____
_____
_____
_____
_____
_____
_____
_____
_____
_____
_____
_____
_____
_____
_____
_____

How did it impact your emotional and mental well-being?

_____
_____
_____
_____
_____
_____
_____
_____
_____
_____
_____
_____
_____

_____

_____

_____

What has your journey to healing looked like so far?

_____

_____

_____

_____

_____

_____

_____

_____

_____

_____

_____

_____

Write about your thoughts and feelings, and consider what you have learned along the way.

_____

_____

_____

_____

_____

_____

_____

_____

_____

_____

_____

_____
_____
_____
_____

Identify your triggers. Stalking and harassment can leave survivors with a range of triggers that can cause anxiety, fear, or other negative emotions. Take some time to identify your triggers, such as a particular place, person, or situation. Once you've identified your triggers, write about how you can manage them, whether it's through avoidance, setting boundaries, or other coping strategies.

_____
_____
_____
_____
_____
_____
_____
_____
_____
_____
_____
_____
_____
_____

Practice gratitude. Stalking and harassment can leave survivors feeling powerless and helpless. It can be difficult to focus on the positive aspects of life when you're dealing with such a challenging experience. Take some time each day to write down three things you're grateful for, no matter how small they may seem. Focusing on the good things in your life can help you build resilience and find hope.

_____

_____

_____

_____

_____

_____

_____

_____

_____

_____

_____

_____

_____

_____

_____

Write a letter to your younger self. For many survivors of stalking and harassment, the experience can be tied to past traumas or difficult experiences. Write a letter to your younger self, offering comfort, support, and advice. Reflect on what you wish you had known when you were going through those challenges, and consider how you can apply those lessons to your current situation.

_____

_____

_____

_____

_____

_____

_____

_____

_____

_____

Set intentions for the future. Stalking and harassment can make it difficult to look ahead with optimism and hope. Take some time to set intentions for the future, whether it's a goal you want to achieve or a positive quality you want to cultivate in yourself. Write about your vision for the future, and consider the steps you can take to move closer to that vision.

CHAPTER 2 UNDERSTANDING STALKING AND HARASSMENT

Definition and types of stalking and harassment
The impact of stalking and harassment on mental health
Statistics and prevalence of stalking and harassment

Stalking and harassment are two of the most pervasive forms of interpersonal violence that many individuals unfortunately face. Whether you are a survivor or just seeking to learn more about the topic, it is crucial to have a comprehensive understanding of the dynamics of stalking and harassment. This chapter seeks to provide that understanding by discussing the definition and types of stalking and harassment, the impact of these experiences on mental health, and statistics and prevalence rates associated with these types of violence.

Stalking is often defined as a pattern of behavior in which an individual repeatedly makes unwanted or threatening contact with another person. This can take many forms, such as following someone, sending unwanted messages, or vandalizing property. The goal of the stalker is often to intimidate or control the victim, leading to feelings of fear, anxiety, and loss of control.

Harassment, on the other hand, is a broader term that encompasses a range of behaviors aimed at creating a hostile or intimidating environment for the victim. This can include verbal abuse, sexual harassment, or discrimination based on race, gender, or sexual orientation. Like stalking, harassment can cause significant psychological harm to the victim, leading to feelings of isolation, depression, and anxiety.

The impact of stalking and harassment on mental health cannot be overstated. Studies have shown that survivors of stalking and harassment are at an increased risk for developing mental health disorders, such as post-traumatic stress disorder (PTSD), depression, and anxiety. The constant fear and uncertainty that come with these experiences can take a toll on the victim's emotional well-being, leading to a range of physical symptoms such as headaches, insomnia, and fatigue.

Unfortunately, stalking and harassment are all too common in our society. According to a 2017 report by the National Center for Victims of Crime, 7.5 million people in the United States are stalked each year, with one in six women experiencing stalking at some point in their lives. Similarly, the Equal Employment Opportunity Commission reports that workplace harassment is a pervasive problem, with over 80% of women reporting that they have experienced harassment in the workplace.

It is clear that stalking and harassment have a significant impact on individuals and society as a whole. Understanding the dynamics of these experiences is the first step towards preventing and addressing this type of violence. In the following chapters, we will explore the various strategies and techniques survivors can use to overcome the impact of stalking and harassment and take back control of their lives.

Definition and types of stalking and harassment

Stalking and harassment are two words that carry so much weight and fear for many of us. They are two words that describe a type of behavior that is not only harmful but often terrifying. As a survivor of stalking and harassment, I understand all too well the impact that these experiences can have on a person's life. In this chapter, we will dive deeper into the definition and types of stalking and harassment, with the aim of providing a better understanding of the dynamics of these experiences.

Stalking is a pattern of unwanted behavior that is directed towards another person. This behavior can take many forms, including following, watching, or tracking the victim's movements. It can also include unwanted phone calls, emails, or text messages. In some cases, stalkers may use technology to monitor their victim's activity, such as installing spyware on their phone or computer. The ultimate goal of the stalker is to exert control over the victim and to make them feel afraid and intimidated.

There are several different types of stalking, including intimate partner stalking, stranger stalking, and celebrity stalking. Intimate partner stalking is the most common type and occurs when a current or former partner engages in stalking behavior towards their significant other. This can include following them, harassing them at work, or monitoring their social media activity. Stranger stalking, on the other hand, is when the stalker has no prior relationship with the victim. Celebrity stalking is another type of stalking that has gained more attention in recent years due to the prevalence of social media. This occurs when an individual becomes fixated on a celebrity and engages in stalking behavior towards them.

Harassment, on the other hand, is a type of behavior that is aimed at creating a hostile or intimidating environment for the victim. This behavior can include verbal abuse, unwanted physical contact, or sexual harassment. Workplace harassment is a type of harassment that occurs in the workplace, often between coworkers or between an employer and employee. This can include sexual harassment, discrimination based on race or gender, or bullying.

It is important to note that stalking and harassment are not mutually exclusive, and many victims may experience both types of behavior. For example, a victim of intimate partner violence may also be experiencing stalking behavior from their abuser.

The impact of stalking and harassment on a victim's life can be profound. The constant fear and uncertainty that comes with being stalked or harassed can lead to feelings of isolation, anxiety, and depression. Victims may also experience physical symptoms, such as headaches or stomach problems, as a result of the stress and fear that these experiences cause.

It is crucial to recognize the signs of stalking and harassment and to take steps to protect yourself if you are experiencing these types of behaviors. This can include talking to a trusted friend or family member, seeking support from a therapist or support group, and taking legal action if necessary.

In the following chapters, we will explore the various strategies and techniques that survivors can use to overcome the impact of stalking and harassment and take back control of their lives. But first, it is important to fully understand the definition and types of stalking and harassment so that we can recognize these behaviors and take steps to protect ourselves.

Journal Entries

Reflect on your own experiences or the experiences of someone you know who has been affected by stalking or harassment. Write about how it made you or them feel, the impact it had on your/their life, and any strategies that were helpful in coping with the experience.

_____

_____

_____

_____

_____

_____

_____

_____

_____

_____

_____

_____

_____

_____

_____

_____

_____

_____

_____

_____

_____

_____

_____

_____

_____

_____

_____

_____

_____

_____

_____

_____

Write a letter to yourself at the beginning of your stalking or harassment experience, offering advice and support that you wish you had received at the time. Reflect on what you have learned since then and how you have grown as a person as a result of the experience.

_____

_____

_____

_____

_____

_____

_____

_____

_____

_____

_____

_____

_____

_____

_____

_____

_____

_____

_____

_____

_____

_____

_____

_____

_____

_____

_____

_____

Create a list of healthy coping mechanisms that you can turn to when you feel overwhelmed or triggered by memories of your stalking or harassment experience. Include things like going for a walk, talking to a friend, or practicing mindfulness.

_____

_____

_____

_____

_____

_____

_____

_____

_____

_____

_____

_____

_____

_____

_____

_____

_____

_____

_____

_____

_____

_____

_____

_____

_____

_____

_____

_____

_____

_____

_____

_____

Consider the different types of stalking and harassment outlined in
Chapter 2. Have you experienced any of these types of behaviors?
Write about how it made you feel and what strategies you used to cope.

Write a letter to a loved one or friend who may be experiencing stalking or harassment. Offer words of support and encouragement, and share any resources or advice that you have found helpful in your own journey.

_____

_____

_____

_____

_____

_____

_____

_____

_____

_____

_____

_____

_____

_____

_____

_____

_____

_____

_____

_____

_____

_____

_____

_____

_____

_____

_____

_____

_____

_____

_____

The impact of stalking and harassment on mental health

Stalking and harassment can have a profound impact on an individual's mental health. As a survivor of these experiences, I can attest to the toll they can take on one's emotional well-being. In this chapter, we will explore the ways in which stalking and harassment can affect mental health and well-being.

The emotional impact of stalking and harassment can be devastating. When someone is being stalked or harassed, they may experience fear, anxiety, and a sense of helplessness. These feelings can be overwhelming and can affect every aspect of one's life. For me, the fear and anxiety that came with being stalked made it difficult to trust others, even those closest to me. I was constantly on edge, worried that I would be followed or that the person stalking me would find me.

Stalking and harassment can also lead to symptoms of depression. When I was being stalked, I often felt like I was trapped in a never-ending cycle of fear and sadness. I withdrew from my friends and family, feeling like I didn't want to burden them with my problems. I struggled with feelings of worthlessness and hopelessness, and it was difficult to see a way out of the situation.

In addition to the emotional impact, stalking and harassment can also have physical effects on one's health. The stress and anxiety caused by being stalked can lead to physical symptoms such as headaches, muscle tension, and digestive issues. I remember feeling physically exhausted all the time, as if I was constantly on high alert and never able to truly relax.

It's important to note that the impact of stalking and harassment on mental health can be long-lasting. Even after the stalking or harassment has stopped, survivors may continue to experience symptoms of anxiety or depression. For me, it took a long time to feel like I could trust others and to feel safe in my own skin again.

Unfortunately, the prevalence of stalking and harassment is all too common. According to the National Intimate Partner and Sexual Violence Survey, 1 in 6 women and 1 in 17 men have experienced stalking in their lifetime. These statistics are staggering, and it's important to remember that survivors of stalking and harassment are not alone.

The good news is that there is help available for those who have experienced stalking or harassment. Seeking support from a therapist or counselor can be a crucial step in healing from the emotional toll of these experiences. It's also important to surround yourself with a strong support system of friends and loved ones who can offer encouragement and support.

In conclusion, the impact of stalking and harassment on mental health cannot be overstated. Survivors may experience a range of emotional and physical symptoms, and it's important to seek help and support in healing from these experiences. Remember that you are not alone, and there is hope for healing and recovery.

Journal Exercices

Reflect on your emotional experience: Take some time to write about your emotional experience of being stalked or harassed. How did it make you feel?

_____

_____

_____

_____

_____

_____

_____

_____

_____

_____

_____

_____

_____

_____

_____

_____

_____

_____

_____

_____

_____

_____

_____

_____

_____

_____

_____

_____

_____

What emotions did you experience most frequently?

_____

_____

_____

_____

_____

_____

_____

How did these emotions impact your daily life?

Explore the physical impact: Consider the physical impact of being stalked or harassed. What physical symptoms did you experience as a result of the stress and anxiety?

_____
_____
_____
_____
_____
_____
_____
_____
_____
_____
_____
_____
_____
_____
_____
_____
_____
_____
_____
_____
_____
_____
_____

How did these physical symptoms impact your daily life?

_____
_____
_____
_____
_____
_____
_____

_____

_____

_____

_____

_____

_____

_____

_____

_____

_____

_____

_____

_____

_____

_____

_____

_____

_____

_____

_____

_____

Consider the long-term impact: Reflect on the long-term impact of being stalked or harassed. Are you still experiencing symptoms of anxiety or depression?

_____

_____

_____

_____

_____

_____

_____

_____

_____

_____

_____

_____

_____

_____

_____

_____

_____

_____

_____

_____

_____

_____

_____

_____

_____

_____

_____

Have you noticed any lingering effects on your mental health or well-being?

_____

_____

_____

_____

_____

_____

_____

_____

_____

_____

_____

_____

_____

_____

_____

_____

_____

_____

_____

_____

_____

_____

_____

_____

_____

_____

_____

_____

_____

Identify your support system: Take some time to think about your
support system. Who has been there for you during this difficult time?

_____

_____

_____

_____

_____

_____

_____

_____

_____

_____

_____

_____

_____

_____

_____

_____

_____

_____

_____

_____

_____

_____

_____

_____

_____

_____

_____

_____

Who can you turn to for encouragement and support?

_____

_____

_____

_____

Write about the ways in which your support system has helped you cope with the impact of stalking and harassment.

_____

_____

_____

_____

_____

_____

_____

_____

_____

_____

_____

_____

_____

_____

_____

_____

_____

_____

_____

_____

_____

_____

_____

_____

_____

_____

_____

Focus on self-care: Finally, consider the importance of self-care in healing from the impact of stalking and harassment. What self-care practices have been helpful for you?

_____

_____

_____

_____

_____

_____

_____

_____

_____

_____

_____

_____

_____

_____

_____

_____

_____

_____

_____

_____

_____

_____

_____

_____

_____

_____

_____

_____

_____

_____

_____

What activities bring you a sense of peace and calm?

_____

_____

Write about the ways in which you prioritize self-care and how it has helped you cope with the emotional toll of these experiences.

Statistics and prevalence of stalking and harassment

As someone who has experienced stalking and harassment firsthand, it is deeply concerning to learn about the prevalence of these behaviors in our society. While it can be difficult to face the statistics, it is important to understand the scope of the problem in order to effectively address it.

According to a study by the National Institute of Justice, approximately 7.5 million people in the United States are stalked each year. That means that one in six women and one in 17 men have experienced stalking at some point in their lives. This number is staggering, and it is clear that stalking is a serious issue that affects a significant portion of our population.

Stalking can take many forms, and it is not always easy to identify. It can include unwanted phone calls, emails, or text messages, as well as following someone, leaving unwanted gifts or notes, and monitoring someone's online activity. Stalking can be a persistent and ongoing behavior that causes immense fear and distress for the victim.

Harassment is another form of unwanted behavior that can have a profound impact on mental health. According to a survey by the Pew Research Center, 41% of women have experienced online harassment, while 17% have experienced severe forms of harassment, such as physical threats or stalking. These behaviors can take many forms, including name-calling, shaming, and threats of violence.

The prevalence of stalking and harassment is not limited to the United States. In fact, a study conducted by the European Union Agency for Fundamental Rights found that one in five women in the European Union has experienced stalking, while 55% have experienced sexual harassment. These numbers are shocking, and they highlight the need for a global effort to combat these harmful behaviors.

It is important to note that the impact of stalking and harassment is not limited to the victim. Friends and family members may also experience the emotional toll of these behaviors, and they may be impacted by the victim's fear and anxiety. In addition, the broader community may be affected by the prevalence of stalking and harassment, as these behaviors can contribute to a culture of fear and mistrust.

While these statistics are concerning, it is important to remember that healing and recovery are possible. By speaking out about our experiences and working to raise awareness about the impact of stalking and harassment, we can help to create a safer and more compassionate world. It is my hope that this book will serve as a resource and a source of support for those who have experienced these behaviors, and that it will help to promote healing and resilience in the face of adversity.

Journal Entries

Reflect on your own experiences: Take some time to reflect on your own experiences with stalking or harassment. What impact did these behaviors have on your mental health and overall well-being?

_____

_____

_____

_____

_____

_____

_____

_____

_____

_____

_____

_____

_____

_____

_____

Did you feel supported by those around you?

Write about your thoughts and feelings, and consider sharing these reflections with a trusted friend or therapist.

_____

_____

_____

_____

_____

_____

_____

_____

_____

_____

_____

_____

_____

Explore your emotions: Reading about the prevalence of stalking and harassment can be overwhelming and triggering. Take some time to explore the emotions that come up for you as you learn more about these issues. Are you feeling angry, sad, scared, or something else entirely?

_____

_____

_____

_____

_____

_____

_____

_____

_____

_____

_____

_____

Write about these emotions and try to identify any patterns or triggers that may be contributing to your feelings.

_____

_____

_____

_____

_____

_____

_____

_____

_____

_____

_____

_____

_____

_____

_____

_____

_____

_____

Consider the broader impact: It's not just victims who are impacted by stalking and harassment – friends, family members, and the broader community may also be affected. Take some time to consider the broader impact of these behaviors on your community, and reflect on any actions you can take to promote safety and support for those who have been impacted.

_____

_____

_____

_____

_____

_____

_____

_____

_____

_____

_____

_____

_____

_____

_____

_____

_____

_____

_____

_____

_____

_____

_____

_____

_____

_____

_____

_____

_____

_____

_____

Identify areas for advocacy: The prevalence of stalking and harassment is a societal issue, and it will take a collective effort to address it. Consider how you can use your voice and resources to advocate for change. This might include sharing your story, supporting organizations that work to prevent and respond to these behaviors, or advocating for policy changes at the local or national level.

_____

_____

Practice self-care: Learning about the prevalence of stalking and harassment can be emotionally taxing. Make sure to prioritize your own self-care as you process these statistics. This might include activities like exercise, meditation, spending time with loved ones, or engaging in creative pursuits. Write about any self-care practices that have been helpful for you in the past, and brainstorm new ideas that you might like to try.

In conclusion, understanding the definition, types, and prevalence of stalking and harassment is crucial for both survivors and those seeking to support them. These behaviors can have a profound impact on mental health and well-being, and it's important to take steps to address them both on an individual and societal level. By recognizing the scope of the issue and advocating for change, we can work towards a world where stalking and harassment are not tolerated, and all individuals feel safe and supported. In the next chapter, we will delve into the complexities of healing from the trauma of stalking and harassment, and provide tools and resources for survivors to begin their journey towards recovery.

CHAPTER 3

Survivor Stories
Personal accounts of stalking and harassment from survivors
Their experiences, emotions, and reactions
How they coped and overcame their experiences

Survivor Stories

Dear Reader,

My name is Alex and I am a survivor of stalking. When I was in my mid-twenties, I met a woman at a local bar. We hit it off right away and started dating. However, things quickly took a turn for the worse. She became possessive and jealous, always wanting to know where I was and who I was with. She started showing up unannounced at my work and my apartment. She would call me incessantly, leaving angry messages when I didn't answer. It felt like there was no escaping her.

I was scared and didn't know what to do. I confided in a friend who urged me to get a restraining order. It was a difficult decision to make, but ultimately it was the best thing I could have done. The process was stressful and scary, but I knew I needed to take action to protect myself.

It's been several years since then, and while the experience was traumatic, it has also taught me a lot about resilience and strength. I hope that by sharing my story, I can inspire others to seek help and take action when they find themselves in similar situations.

Sincerely,
Alex

Dear Reader,

My name is Sarah and I am a survivor of harassment. When I was in college, I had a professor who made inappropriate comments and advances towards me. It started off innocently enough - compliments on my appearance, invitations to dinner - but soon escalated to unwelcome touching and lewd remarks.

I was terrified and didn't know what to do. I didn't want to jeopardize my academic career, so I tried to ignore it and hope it would go away. But it only got worse. I started skipping class and avoiding the professor, but he would find ways to contact me - through email, social media, and even showing up at my dorm.

It took a toll on my mental health and I felt like I had nowhere to turn. Finally, I confided in a friend who urged me to report the professor to the school. It was a difficult decision, but ultimately the right one. The school took my report seriously and the professor was fired.

It's been several years since then, but the experience still haunts me. However, I am grateful for the support of my friends and the resources available to me. I hope that by sharing my story, I can encourage others to speak out and seek help when they experience harassment.

Sincerely,
Sarah

Personal accounts of stalking and harassment from survivors

As a survivor of stalking and harassment, I know how it feels to have your life turned upside down. It's a traumatic experience that can leave deep emotional scars, affecting every aspect of your life. That's why it's important to share personal accounts of stalking and harassment from survivors. By doing so, we can help others understand the impact of this crime and support those who have been through it.

One survivor's story is that of Jane, who was stalked by her ex-boyfriend for months after they broke up. He would show up unannounced at her home and work, send her endless texts and emails, and leave threatening voicemails. She lived in constant fear, always looking over her shoulder and wondering if he was watching her. It took a toll on her mental health, and she struggled to maintain her job and relationships.

Another survivor is James, who was harassed by a former colleague at work. The colleague would make derogatory comments about his race and sexual orientation, and spread false rumors about him to other coworkers. James felt isolated and vulnerable, and feared that his job would be at risk if he spoke up. He eventually found the courage to report the harassment and was able to get the support he needed.

These personal accounts are just two examples of the many experiences that survivors of stalking and harassment face. Each story is unique, but they all share a common thread of trauma and pain. It's important that we listen to these stories with empathy and understanding, and work towards creating a world where stalking and harassment are not tolerated.

Survivors of stalking and harassment need to know that they are not alone. By sharing our stories, we can break the silence and build a community of support. We can also raise awareness of this crime and advocate for stronger laws and policies to prevent it from happening in the first place.

To those who are going through this experience, know that you are not to blame for what has happened to you. You deserve to be heard, believed, and supported. There is hope for healing and recovery, and together we can create a future where stalking and harassment are no longer a threat to our safety and wellbeing.

Their experiences, emotions, and reactions

As survivors of stalking and harassment, our experiences, emotions, and reactions are unique and varied. However, there are common threads that bind us together, and by sharing our stories, we can create a sense of solidarity and understanding.

For me, the experience of being stalked and harassed was a constant state of fear and anxiety. I never knew when my stalker would show up or what he would do, and this uncertainty weighed heavily on my mind. I was constantly looking over my shoulder and second-guessing my every move.

At the same time, I felt ashamed and embarrassed about what was happening to me. I blamed myself for not being able to stop it or for somehow bringing it on myself. I didn't want to talk about it with anyone because I didn't want to be judged or labeled as a victim.

But eventually, I realized that keeping it all bottled up was only making things worse. I sought therapy and opened up to close friends and family members. I found that talking about my experiences helped me process my emotions and gain a sense of control over my life again.

One of the most challenging aspects of being a survivor of stalking and harassment is the emotional toll it takes on us. We may experience a range of emotions, from fear and anger to sadness and despair. It's important to acknowledge and validate these emotions and not try to suppress them.

Some survivors may also struggle with trust issues and feel like they can never fully let their guard down again. It's important to take things at our own pace and recognize that healing is a process, not a destination.

Another common reaction among survivors is a sense of isolation and feeling like no one understands what we're going through. But by connecting with other survivors and sharing our stories, we can break down these barriers and create a supportive community.

It's also worth noting that the impact of stalking and harassment is not limited to the immediate aftermath. For many survivors, the trauma can linger for years, impacting our relationships, careers, and overall well-being.

But by sharing our stories and working through our emotions, we can begin to heal and move forward. It's a difficult journey, but one that is worth taking.

As survivors, we have a unique perspective that can help others who may be going through similar experiences. By speaking out and raising awareness, we can help prevent others from experiencing the same trauma that we have endured.

Remember, you are not alone, and there is hope for healing and recovery.

Journal Exercises

Reflect on a time when you or someone you know experienced stalking or harassment. What were the emotions and reactions that you or they had during this experience?

_____
_____
_____
_____
_____
_____
_____
_____
_____

How did it affect your/their mental and emotional well-being?

Write down your thoughts and feelings in your journal.

_____

_____

_____

_____

_____

_____

_____

_____

_____

_____

_____

_____

_____

_____

_____

_____

_____

_____

Imagine you are a survivor of stalking or harassment. Write a letter to your younger self, offering support and advice for dealing with the experience. What would you say to comfort and empower yourself during this difficult time?

_____

_____

_____

_____

_____

_____

_____

_____

_____

_____

_____

_____

_____

_____

_____

_____

_____

_____

_____

_____

_____

_____

_____

_____

_____

_____

_____

_____

_____

_____

Write down three things that you would say to someone who has just experienced stalking or harassment. What words of comfort and advice would you offer?

_____

_____

_____

_____

_____

_____

_____

_____

_____

_____

_____

_____

_____

_____

_____

_____

_____

_____

_____

_____

_____

_____

_____

_____

_____

_____

_____

_____

_____

How would you encourage them to take care of their mental and emotional health?

_____

_____

_____

_____

_____

_____

_____

_____

_____

_____

_____

_____

_____

_____

_____

_____

_____

_____

_____

_____

_____

_____

_____

_____

_____

_____

_____

_____

_____

_____

_____

Think about the ways in which survivors of stalking and harassment often blame themselves or feel ashamed of their experiences. Write down any thoughts or feelings you have around this topic. How can we work to shift the blame from survivors to the perpetrators of these crimes?

Take some time to reflect on the personal accounts of stalking and harassment shared in this chapter. What can we learn from these stories? How can we support survivors of these experiences?

_____

_____

_____

_____

_____

_____

_____

_____

_____

_____

_____

_____

_____

_____

_____

_____

_____

_____

_____

_____

_____

_____

_____

_____

_____

_____

_____

_____

_____

_____

_____

_____

Write down any insights or ideas you have in your journal.

_____

_____

_____

_____

How they coped and overcame their experiences

When you experience stalking or harassment, it can be incredibly difficult to cope with the trauma and aftermath. However, many survivors find ways to cope, heal, and eventually overcome their experiences. In this chapter, I'll share personal stories of how survivors coped with their experiences and eventually found healing.

One survivor, Claire, found that journaling was a helpful coping mechanism. She began writing down her thoughts and feelings about her experience of being stalked, which allowed her to process her emotions in a healthy way. Over time, she was able to work through her trauma and regain a sense of control over her life.

Another survivor, Jason, found that therapy was an essential part of his healing journey. He sought out a therapist who specialized in working with survivors of stalking and harassment, and together they worked through the trauma he had experienced. With the support of his therapist and loved ones, he was eventually able to move past his experience and begin to rebuild his life.

For many survivors, finding a sense of community and support was crucial in their healing process. Sarah, for example, joined a survivor support group and found comfort in connecting with others who had experienced similar trauma. Through sharing her story with others and receiving support from the group, she was able to find a sense of validation and healing.

Some survivors also found that engaging in creative pursuits, such as writing, painting, or music, was a helpful way to cope with their experiences. Beth, for example, began writing a memoir about her experience of being stalked, which allowed her to reclaim her narrative and find a sense of purpose in her trauma.

Ultimately, there is no one "right" way to cope with stalking and harassment. Every survivor's journey is unique, and what works for one person may not work for another. However, what is important is that survivors have access to the resources and support they need to heal and move forward.

If you are a survivor of stalking or harassment, know that healing is possible. It may take time, effort, and support, but with perseverance and self-care, it is possible to overcome the trauma and find a sense of peace and empowerment. Remember that you are not alone, and that there are resources available to help you on your healing journey.

Journal Exercises

Reflect on your own coping mechanisms: Take some time to think about how you typically cope with stress and difficult emotions. Do you have healthy coping mechanisms, or are there areas where you could improve?

_____

_____

_____

_____

_____

_____

_____

_____

_____

_____

_____

_____

_____

_____

_____

_____

_____

_____

_____

_____

_____

_____

_____

_____

_____

_____

_____

_____

_____

What are some new coping strategies you could try to help you overcome difficult experiences?

_____

_____

_____

_____

_____

_____

_____

_____

_____

_____

_____

_____

_____

_____

_____

_____

_____

_____

_____

_____

_____

_____

_____

_____

_____

_____

_____

_____

_____

_____

_____

Write about a time when you overcame a difficult experience: Think about a challenging situation you have faced in the past. How did you cope with it, and what strategies did you use to overcome it?

_____

_____

_____

_____

_____

_____

_____

_____

_____

_____

_____

_____

_____

_____

_____

_____

_____

_____

_____

_____

_____

_____

_____

_____

_____

_____

_____

_____

_____

Reflect on what you learned from the experience and how you could apply those lessons to future challenges.

Brainstorm a list of positive affirmations: Write down a list of positive affirmations you can use to remind yourself of your strength and resilience. For example, "I am capable of overcoming challenges," "I am worthy of love and respect," or "I am strong and resilient."

_____

_____

_____

_____

_____

_____

_____

_____

_____

_____

_____

_____

_____

_____

_____

_____

_____

_____

_____

_____

_____

_____

_____

_____

_____

_____

_____

_____

_____

_____

Practice self-care: Think about some ways you can practice self-care to help you cope with difficult experiences. This might include things like taking a bubble bath, going for a walk in nature, practicing meditation or yoga, or spending time with loved ones.

_____

_____

_____

_____

_____

_____

_____

_____

_____

_____

_____

_____

_____

_____

_____

_____

_____

_____

_____

_____

_____

_____

_____

_____

_____

_____

_____

_____

_____

_____

_____

Set goals for the future: Think about some goals you would like to achieve in the future, whether they are related to your personal or professional life. Write them down and think about what steps you can take to work towards them.

_____

_____

_____

_____

_____

_____

_____

_____

_____

_____

_____

_____

_____

_____

_____

_____

_____

_____

_____

_____

_____

_____

_____

_____

_____

_____

_____

_____

_____

_____

Conclusion :

In this chapter, we have heard from survivors of stalking and harassment about their experiences, emotions, reactions, and coping strategies. We have seen that each survivor's journey is unique, but that there are common themes of fear, shame, and isolation. We have also seen that there are many ways to cope with and overcome difficult experiences, from therapy and self-care to seeking support from loved ones and taking action to protect oneself.

While healing from stalking and harassment can be a long and difficult journey, it is important to remember that healing is possible. Survivors have shown incredible strength and resilience in the face of adversity, and their stories serve as a testament to the human capacity for healing and growth. In the next chapter, we will explore the legal and practical aspects of dealing with stalking and harassment, and how survivors can take action to protect themselves and seek justice.

CHAPTER 4 WARNING SIGNS AND PREVENTION

Introduction
Recognizing the warning signs of stalking and harassment
Understanding how to prevent it from happening
Practical tips for staying safe
Conclusion

Introduction

As a survivor of stalking and harassment, the topic of recognizing warning signs and preventing these behaviors hits close to home for me. In this chapter, we will explore the different warning signs of stalking and harassment, and what steps we can take to prevent these behaviors from happening in the first place.

It's important to acknowledge that stalking and harassment can happen to anyone, regardless of age, gender, or social status. These behaviors can range from unwanted messages and phone calls to physical violence, and can have a devastating impact on our mental health and overall well-being.

Recognizing the warning signs of stalking and harassment is crucial in preventing it from escalating to a dangerous level. We need to be aware of red flags such as persistent messages or calls, unwanted gifts, and following or monitoring our movements. By understanding these warning signs, we can take proactive steps to protect ourselves and seek help when needed.

In addition to recognizing warning signs, prevention is key in stopping stalking and harassment before it starts. This includes taking steps such as setting clear boundaries with others, being mindful of what personal information we share online, and seeking help from trusted sources such as friends, family, or professional support.

It's also important to acknowledge that prevention isn't always foolproof, and that no one is to blame for being a victim of stalking or harassment. However, by taking steps to prevent these behaviors and recognizing warning signs, we can empower ourselves and reduce the likelihood of experiencing these traumatic experiences.

In this chapter, we will explore practical tips and strategies for recognizing warning signs and preventing stalking and harassment, as well as resources for seeking help and support. By working together and sharing our experiences, we can create a safer and more supportive community for survivors of stalking and harassment.

Brief overview of the chapter's focus on warning signs and prevention of stalking and harassment

As survivors of stalking and harassment, we know all too well the devastating impact these behaviors can have on our lives. From the fear and anxiety that pervade our thoughts and emotions, to the physical toll it can take on our bodies, stalking and harassment can feel all-encompassing and overwhelming. But the good news is that there are steps we can take to recognize and prevent these behaviors from happening to us or our loved ones.

In this chapter, we will explore the warning signs of stalking and harassment, how to prevent it from happening, and practical tips for staying safe. By understanding the red flags of these behaviors, we can take proactive steps to protect ourselves and others from the trauma and pain that stalking and harassment can cause.

It's important to recognize that stalking and harassment can take many different forms, and that it's not always easy to spot the warning signs. That's why this chapter will provide a comprehensive overview of the different types of behaviors that fall under the umbrella of stalking and harassment, and what to look out for in order to stay safe.

We will also delve into the psychological and emotional factors that can contribute to stalking and harassment, including the role of power and control in these behaviors. By understanding the motivations behind these actions, we can better equip ourselves to recognize and prevent them from happening.

Most importantly, this chapter will provide practical tips and tools for staying safe in the face of stalking and harassment. From setting boundaries with friends and acquaintances, to navigating the legal system if necessary, we will explore the steps we can take to protect ourselves and our loved ones from these harmful behaviors.

At the end of this chapter, I hope you will feel empowered and equipped with the knowledge and tools to recognize and prevent stalking and harassment from happening in your life. While we cannot control the actions of others, we can control our own responses and actions, and take proactive steps to stay safe and protect our well-being.

Journal Exercises

Self-Assessment: Take some time to reflect on your own experiences with potentially concerning behavior from others. Write about a time when you felt uneasy or unsafe around someone, and try to identify specific behaviors or actions that made you feel that way. Were there any warning signs that you missed?

_____

_____

_____

_____

_____

What could you have done differently to protect yourself?

_____

_____

_____

_____

_____

_____

_____

_____

_____

_____

_____

_____

_____

_____

_____

_____

_____

_____

_____

_____

_____

_____

_____

_____

_____

Scenarios: Write about several different scenarios that might involve stalking or harassment. For example, someone you've just met starts messaging you constantly and asking personal questions, or someone you used to date keeps showing up unexpectedly at places you go. For each scenario, identify any warning signs that might indicate that the behavior is problematic, and brainstorm some strategies for how you could respond if the behavior continues.

_____

_____

_____

_____

_____

_____

_____

_____

_____

_____

_____

_____

_____

_____

_____

_____

_____

_____

_____

_____

_____

_____

_____

_____

_____

_____

_____

_____

_____

_____

_____

Personal Boundaries: Think about your own personal boundaries and what you are and aren't comfortable with when it comes to interacting with others. Write down some of your personal rules and boundaries, such as not giving out your phone number to strangers or not agreeing to meet someone alone for the first time. Consider whether these boundaries are realistic and effective, and think about whether there are any additional boundaries you should set for yourself.

_____

_____

_____

_____

_____

_____

_____

_____

Prevention Strategies: Brainstorm some practical strategies for preventing stalking and harassment, such as varying your routine, limiting the amount of personal information you share online, or using a buddy system when going out. Write about which strategies seem most feasible and effective for you, and consider how you could incorporate them into your daily life.

_____

_____

_____

_____

_____

_____

_____

_____

_____

_____

_____

_____

_____

_____

_____

_____

_____

_____

_____

_____

_____

_____

_____

_____

_____

_____

_____

_____

_____

_____

Seeking Help: Write about the barriers that might prevent you from seeking help if you were being stalked or harassed, such as fear of not being believed or concerns about retaliation. Identify some strategies for overcoming these barriers, such as confiding in a trusted friend or family member, seeking support from a professional, or reporting the behavior to law enforcement.

_____

_____

_____

_____

_____

_____

_____

_____

_____

_____

_____

_____

_____

_____
_____
_____
_____
_____
_____
_____
_____
_____
_____
_____
_____
_____
_____
_____
_____
_____
_____

Importance of recognizing and preventing these behaviors

Stalking and harassment can have a profound and lasting impact on a person's mental health and well-being. It's important to recognize and prevent these behaviors before they escalate and cause further harm. In this chapter, we'll explore the importance of recognizing warning signs and taking proactive steps to prevent stalking and harassment.

As a survivor of stalking and harassment, I understand firsthand the importance of recognizing these behaviors early on. It can be easy to dismiss seemingly harmless actions, such as a few unwanted messages or phone calls, as simply annoying or inconvenient. But it's important to remember that these actions can quickly escalate and become more dangerous if left unchecked.

One of the key aspects of recognizing warning signs is understanding the different forms that stalking and harassment can take. These behaviors can range from persistent unwanted contact, such as emails or phone calls, to physical stalking, including following or spying on a person. It's important to be aware of these behaviors and take them seriously, even if they seem minor at first.

Another important aspect of recognizing warning signs is understanding the motivations behind these behaviors. Stalking and harassment can be motivated by a variety of factors, including a desire for control or power over another person, a romantic or sexual obsession, or a desire for revenge or retaliation. By understanding these motivations, we can better identify warning signs and take steps to protect ourselves.

Prevention is also a crucial aspect of addressing stalking and harassment. There are many practical steps that individuals can take to protect themselves from these behaviors, including changing their routines, securing their homes, and being mindful of their online presence. It's also important to seek support from friends, family, or professionals if you feel that you are being targeted.

It's important to remember that no one deserves to be the victim of stalking or harassment, and there are resources and support available for those who have experienced these behaviors. By recognizing warning signs early on and taking proactive steps to prevent stalking and harassment, we can empower ourselves and take control of our safety and well-being.

As you reflect on the importance of recognizing and preventing stalking and harassment, consider the following journal prompts:

Have you ever experienced any warning signs of stalking or harassment? How did you react to these behaviors?

What are some practical steps you can take to protect yourself from stalking and harassment?

How can you educate yourself and others about the warning signs and impact of stalking and harassment?

Reflect on a time when you felt particularly vulnerable or unsafe. What steps did you take to protect yourself in that situation?

What resources or support systems are available to you if you experience stalking or harassment in the future? How can you access these resources if needed?

In the next section of this chapter, we'll explore specific warning signs to be aware of and practical tips for preventing stalking and harassment.

Journal Exercises

Reflect on a time when you may have ignored warning signs of stalking or harassment. How did you feel during that experience?

_____

_____

_____

_____

_____

_____

_____

_____

_____

_____

_____

_____

_____

_____

What actions could you have taken to prevent the behavior from
continuing or escalating?

Think about someone you care about who may be experiencing stalking or harassment. What warning signs have you noticed, and how can you approach the situation in a supportive and helpful way?

_____

_____

_____

_____

_____

_____

_____

_____

_____

_____

_____

_____

_____

_____

_____

_____

_____

_____

_____

Write about a time when you took proactive steps to prevent stalking or harassment in your life. How did you feel after taking those actions, and what did you learn from the experience?

_____

_____

_____

_____

_____

_____

_____

_____

_____

Brainstorm a list of practical tips for staying safe from stalking and harassment. Include both physical safety measures and ways to protect your mental health and well-being.

Consider how societal attitudes towards stalking and harassment can contribute to the problem. Write about ways that you can challenge and change harmful beliefs and behaviors related to stalking and harassment in your own life and community.

Recognizing the warning signs of stalking and harassment

Stalking and harassment can be difficult to detect, especially in the early stages. Perpetrators often use subtle tactics to gain control over their victims, which can escalate into more dangerous behaviors over time. It's important to recognize the warning signs early on to prevent further harm. In this chapter, we will explore common warning signs of stalking and harassment, including unwanted communication, surveillance, and unwanted gifts or messages. We'll also discuss the importance of trusting one's instincts and seeking help if suspicious behavior is observed. By recognizing these warning signs and taking action, we can prevent potentially dangerous situations from escalating.

Examples of common warning signs such as unwanted communication, surveillance, and unwanted gifts or messages

Unwanted Communication:

➤ Repeatedly calling, texting, or emailing even after being asked to stop
➤ Sending unsolicited letters or packages
➤ Leaving unwanted notes or messages on social media or online forums
➤ Making inappropriate or threatening comments
➤ Surveillance:

➤ Following or watching the victim, either in person or online
➤ Using GPS trackers or other technology to monitor the victim's movements
➤ Frequently showing up in places the victim frequents, such as their workplace or favorite coffee shop
➤ Gathering information about the victim through friends, family, or social media

Unwanted Gifts or Messages:

➢ Sending unsolicited gifts, such as flowers or jewelry
➢ Leaving notes or messages at the victim's home or workplace
➢ Using social media or other online platforms to send unwanted messages or comments
➢ Making unwanted advances or expressing romantic or sexual interest despite being rejected
➢ It's important to note that these warning signs may not always be obvious or explicit. Stalkers and harassers may try to disguise their behavior as innocent or well-intentioned, which is why it's crucial to trust your instincts and seek help if you feel uncomfortable or suspicious.

Discussion of the importance of trusting one's instincts and seeking help if suspicious behavior is observed

Trusting one's instincts and seeking help are critical when it comes to recognizing and preventing stalking and harassment. Unfortunately, many survivors often ignore or downplay the warning signs, dismissing them as insignificant or imagining things. This is understandable given that stalkers and harassers are often skilled at gaslighting and manipulating their victims, making them question their own perceptions and reality.

However, ignoring these warning signs can lead to serious consequences, including physical harm, emotional trauma, and even death. It's essential to trust your instincts and take any suspicious behavior seriously, no matter how minor it may seem.

One of the most common warning signs of stalking and harassment is unwanted communication. This can take many forms, such as text messages, phone calls, emails, or social media messages. The messages may be persistent, frequent, or inappropriate. Stalkers and harassers may also use different numbers or email addresses to contact their victims, making it harder for them to block or ignore them.

Another warning sign is surveillance. This can include being followed or watched, having your home or workplace surveilled, or having your online activity monitored. Stalkers and harassers may also show up unexpectedly at places you frequent, such as the gym or the grocery store. They may also ask mutual friends or acquaintances about your whereabouts or activities.

Unwanted gifts or messages are also a common warning sign. These may include flowers, letters, or other items that are left at your home or workplace without your consent. The messages may be romantic or threatening in nature, and may indicate an obsession or fixation with the victim.

Other warning signs include someone appearing uninvited and unannounced at your home or workplace, someone tampering with your property or possessions, or someone threatening you or your loved ones. It's essential to take these warning signs seriously and seek help if you notice any of them.

Trusting your instincts is crucial when it comes to recognizing and preventing stalking and harassment. If something feels off or suspicious, it's important to listen to that feeling and take steps to protect yourself. This may include contacting law enforcement, seeking a restraining order, or reaching out to a support network for help.

In addition to trusting your instincts, seeking help is also critical. It can be challenging to speak out about being stalked or harassed, especially if you fear that you won't be believed or that the situation will escalate. However, reaching out for help is essential to your safety and well-being. This may involve speaking to law enforcement, a therapist, or a support group.

Remember, stalking and harassment are not your fault, and you have the right to feel safe and secure. Trust your instincts, seek help, and take steps to protect yourself from these dangerous behaviors.

Journal Exercises

Reflect on a time when you felt uncomfortable or suspicious about someone's behavior towards you. What were the warning signs that made you feel this way?

_____

_____

_____

_____

_____

_____

_____

_____

_____

_____

_____

_____

_____

_____

_____

_____

_____

_____

_____

_____

_____

_____

_____

_____

Did you trust your instincts and seek help? Why or why not?

Write down a list of people in your life who you feel safe with and who you could turn to if you were ever in a situation where you felt unsafe or threatened. How would you approach them for help?

_____

_____

_____

_____

_____

_____

Think about a time when you observed suspicious behavior towards
someone else. Did you speak up or report it to someone? If not, what
held you back?

_____

_____

_____

_____

_____

_____

_____

_____

_____

_____

_____

_____

_____

_____

_____

_____

_____

_____

_____

_____

_____

Make a plan for what you would do if you were ever in a situation where you felt unsafe or threatened. This could include identifying safe places to go, people to call for help, and steps you can take to protect yourself.

_____

_____

_____

_____

_____

_____

_____

_____

_____

_____

Write a letter to your future self, reminding yourself to always trust your instincts and seek help if you ever feel threatened or unsafe. What steps can you take to protect yourself and stay safe in these situations? Remember, journaling can be a helpful tool for self-reflection and personal growth. Take the time to reflect on your thoughts and feelings, and be kind and compassionate towards yourself as you navigate these difficult topics.

_____

_____

_____

_____

_____

_____

_____

_____

_____

_____

_____

_____

_____

_____

_____

_____
_____
_____
_____
_____
_____
_____
_____
_____
_____
_____
_____
_____
_____
_____
_____
_____

Understanding how to prevent it from happening

As a survivor of stalking and harassment, I have learned firsthand the importance of understanding how to prevent these behaviors from happening. While it is impossible to completely eliminate the risk of being targeted, there are practical steps that can be taken to reduce the likelihood of being stalked or harassed. In this chapter, I will share my insights and experiences on how to stay safe and protect oneself.

One of the most important aspects of prevention is being aware of one's surroundings and taking measures to ensure personal safety. This includes being mindful of the people around you, particularly in unfamiliar or isolated locations. It is also important to trust one's instincts - if something feels off or suspicious, it is better to be safe than sorry.

Another key aspect of prevention is protecting one's personal information and online presence. This includes being cautious about sharing personal information on social media and other online platforms, as well as using strong passwords and enabling privacy settings. It is also important to be vigilant about potential phishing attempts or other online scams that can compromise personal information.

In addition, having a support system in place can be critical in preventing stalking and harassment. This can include friends, family, and even coworkers who can provide emotional support and help monitor for any suspicious behavior. It is also important to seek professional help if needed, such as consulting with a therapist or legal expert.

Ultimately, prevention requires a combination of vigilance, caution, and support. By taking proactive steps to protect oneself and recognizing warning signs, individuals can reduce the risk of being targeted by stalkers and harassers.

As a survivor, I know firsthand the devastating impact that stalking and harassment can have. It is not something to be taken lightly, and prevention is key in ensuring personal safety and well-being. By following these tips and staying vigilant, we can all work towards a safer and more secure future.

Journal Exercises

Reflect on your personal boundaries: Take some time to reflect on your personal boundaries and what makes you uncomfortable. Write down what behaviors, actions, or words make you feel uncomfortable or uneasy. This exercise can help you identify potential warning signs early on and be proactive about setting boundaries.

_____

_____

_____

_____

_____

Brainstorm ways to protect your privacy: Consider ways to protect your personal information and online presence. Write down a list of steps you can take, such as setting your social media profiles to private, using a strong password, and being cautious about who you share your personal information with.

Identify your support system: Identify the people in your life who you can trust and rely on for support in case you experience stalking or harassment. Write down their names and contact information. This exercise can help you feel more prepared and supported in case of an emergency.

_____

_____

_____

_____

_____

_____

_____

_____

_____

_____

_____

_____

_____

_____

_____

_____

_____

_____

_____

_____

_____

_____

_____

_____

_____

_____

_____

_____

_____

_____

_____

_____

Plan a safety strategy: Develop a safety plan in case you feel threatened or unsafe. Write down the steps you can take, such as calling a trusted friend or family member, contacting law enforcement, or seeking medical attention. This exercise can help you feel more in control and prepared if you ever find yourself in a dangerous situation.

_____

_____

_____

_____

_____

_____

_____

_____

_____

_____

_____

_____

_____

_____

_____

_____

_____

_____

_____

_____

_____

_____

_____

Practice self-care: Coping with the impact of stalking and harassment can be overwhelming and stressful. Write down a list of self-care activities you can do to help manage stress and maintain your mental health. This could include activities such as meditation, exercise, spending time with loved ones, or seeking professional support from a therapist.

_____
_____
_____
_____
_____
_____
_____
_____
_____
_____
_____
_____
_____
_____
_____

Remember, if you are experiencing stalking or harassment, it's important to reach out for help and support. Don't hesitate to contact law enforcement or seek assistance from a professional.

Tips for protecting one's personal information and online presence

❖ Use strong and unique passwords for all online accounts.
❖ Enable two-factor authentication for added security.
❖ Be cautious about sharing personal information online, including on social media platforms.
❖ Avoid clicking on suspicious links or downloading attachments from unknown sources.
❖ Use antivirus software and keep it up to date.
❖ Regularly update the operating system and software on all devices.
❖ Be wary of public Wi-Fi networks and avoid using them for sensitive activities.
❖ Consider using a virtual private network (VPN) when accessing the internet.

- Use privacy settings on social media and other online accounts to control who can see your information.
- Monitor your credit report and financial accounts regularly for any unauthorized activity.
- Don't give out personal information over the phone or in response to unsolicited emails or messages.
- Be cautious of phishing attempts and always verify the legitimacy of requests for personal information.
- By following these tips, individuals can take proactive steps to protect their personal information and online presence from potential threats.

Advice for setting boundaries and communicating effectively with others

As a survivor of stalking and harassment, I know all too well how important it is to set boundaries and communicate effectively with others. In this chapter, I'll share my own experiences and provide advice for others who may be struggling with these issues.

When it comes to setting boundaries, the first step is to identify what your boundaries are. This can be difficult, especially if you've never really thought about it before. For me, it took some time to figure out what my own boundaries were and to learn how to communicate them to others.

One of the most important things I learned is that it's okay to say no. This can be hard, especially if you're someone who tends to be a people pleaser or if you're worried about hurting someone's feelings. But saying no is crucial for setting boundaries and protecting yourself.

Another important aspect of setting boundaries is to be clear and consistent. If you're not consistent in enforcing your boundaries, others may not take them seriously. It's also important to communicate your boundaries in a clear and direct way, rather than expecting others to read your mind.

When it comes to communicating effectively with others, there are a few key things to keep in mind. First, try to be assertive rather than aggressive or passive. Being assertive means standing up for yourself and communicating your needs and feelings in a clear and direct way, while still respecting the other person.

It's also important to listen actively when communicating with others. This means paying attention to what the other person is saying, asking questions, and showing empathy and understanding.

In addition to setting boundaries and communicating effectively, there are other steps you can take to protect yourself from stalking and harassment. One of the most important is to be aware of your surroundings and trust your instincts. If something doesn't feel right, it probably isn't.

It's also important to protect your personal information and online presence. This can include things like using strong passwords, avoiding oversharing on social media, and being cautious when giving out personal information.

Finally, it's important to have a support system in place. This can include friends, family, or a therapist. Having people you can turn to for support can be crucial when dealing with stalking and harassment.

In conclusion, setting boundaries and communicating effectively are crucial for preventing and dealing with stalking and harassment. By identifying your boundaries, being clear and consistent, and communicating assertively, you can protect yourself and take control of your situation. Remember to trust your instincts, protect your personal information, and lean on your support system for help and guidance.

Journal Exercises

Reflect on a time when you felt uncomfortable or violated by someone's behavior towards you. What boundaries could you have set in that situation to communicate your discomfort and protect yourself?

_____

_____

_____

_____

_____

_____

_____

_____

_____

_____

_____

_____

_____

_____

_____

_____

_____

_____

_____

_____

_____

_____

_____

_____

_____

_____

Write about how you could have approached the situation differently, and what you would do differently in the future.

_____

_____

_____

_____

Write down five scenarios in which you might need to set boundaries with someone, whether it's a coworker, friend, or family member. For each scenario, brainstorm ways you can communicate your boundaries effectively and maintain them.

_____

_____

_____

_____

_____

_____

_____

_____

_____

_____

_____

_____

_____

_____

_____

_____

_____

_____

_____

_____

_____

_____

_____

_____

_____

_____

_____

_____

_____

_____

Think about a time when you communicated a boundary to someone and it was not respected. How did you handle the situation, and what could you have done differently? Write about what you learned from that experience and how you can apply it to future situations.

_____

_____

_____

_____

_____

_____

_____

_____

_____

_____

_____

_____

_____

_____

_____

_____

_____

_____

_____

_____

_____

_____

_____

_____

_____

_____

_____

_____

_____

Write a letter to yourself from the perspective of a close friend or family member who has witnessed you struggling to set boundaries in relationships. What advice would they give you?

_____

_____

_____

_____

_____

_____

_____

_____

_____

_____

_____

_____

_____

_____

_____

_____

_____

_____

_____

_____

_____

_____

_____

_____

_____

_____

_____

_____

_____

How can you use their perspective to help you communicate more effectively and protect your own well-being?

_____

_____

_____

_____

_____

_____

_____

_____

_____

_____

_____

_____

_____

_____

_____

_____

_____

_____

_____

_____

_____

_____

_____

_____

_____

_____

_____

_____

_____

_____

Make a list of personal values that are important to you, such as respect, honesty, or independence. How can you use these values to guide your communication and boundary-setting with others? Write about specific actions you can take to honor your values and protect your boundaries.

_____

_____

_____

_____

_____

_____

_____

_____

_____

_____

_____

_____

_____

_____

_____

_____

_____

_____

_____

_____

_____

_____

_____

_____

_____

_____

_____

_____

_____

_____

Reflect on a time when you felt pressure to compromise your boundaries in order to please someone else or avoid conflict. What did you learn from that experience? How can you prioritize your own needs and values while still maintaining positive relationships with others?

_____

_____

_____

_____

_____

_____

_____

_____

_____

_____

Identify three people in your life who you feel comfortable communicating with and who respect your boundaries. Write about why these relationships feel safe and supportive, and how you can strengthen these connections moving forward.

_____

_____

_____

_____

_____

_____

_____

_____

_____

_____

_____

_____

_____

_____

_____

_____

_____

_____

_____

_____

_____

_____

_____

_____

Discussion of the importance of seeking legal help and reporting instances of stalking or harassment

As a survivor of stalking and harassment, one of the most important things I learned was the value of seeking legal help and reporting instances of stalking or harassment. It can be intimidating to take legal action, but it is essential for protecting yourself and preventing the behavior from continuing.

When you experience stalking or harassment, it's important to document everything. Keep a record of any communication, whether it be emails, text messages, voicemails, or letters. Take screenshots of any social media messages or posts related to the harassment. Write down any details about the harassment, including dates, times, and specific incidents. This documentation can be crucial in building a case against the perpetrator.

It's also important to seek out legal help early on. Contacting a lawyer who specializes in stalking or harassment cases can help you understand your legal options and make informed decisions about how to proceed. They can also help you obtain restraining orders or file police reports, if necessary.

Reporting instances of stalking or harassment to law enforcement is another crucial step in protecting yourself. Although it can be difficult to involve the police, it's important to remember that they are there to help and protect you. When you report the behavior, be sure to provide as much detail as possible and provide any evidence you have collected.

Unfortunately, many survivors of stalking or harassment may face challenges when trying to get help. Law enforcement and legal systems are not always supportive or effective in responding to these cases. It's important to seek out advocates or support groups who can help guide you through the process and provide emotional support.

Remember that seeking legal help and reporting instances of stalking or harassment is not just about protecting yourself, but also about preventing the behavior from continuing and protecting others from experiencing it. It can be a difficult and intimidating process, but it is essential for your safety and well-being.

In conclusion, if you are experiencing stalking or harassment, it's important to seek legal help and report the behavior to law enforcement. Document everything, seek out advocates or support groups for help, and remember that you are not alone. Taking these steps can help protect you and prevent the behavior from continuing, and can help send a message that stalking and harassment will not be tolerated.

Journal Exercises

Have you ever experienced or witnessed any instances of stalking or harassment?

_____

_____

_____

_____

_____

_____

_____

_____

_____

_____

_____

_____

_____

_____

_____

_____

_____

_____

_____

_____

_____

_____

_____

How did you or the person involved handle the situation?

_____

_____

_____

_____

_____

_____

_____

_____

What steps could have been taken to prevent it from happening or to seek legal help if necessary?

_____

_____

_____

_____

_____

_____

_____

_____

_____

_____

_____

_____

_____

_____

_____

_____

_____

_____

_____

_____

Think about the legal resources available in your community or country for victims of stalking and harassment. Research and write down the contact information for these resources in case you or someone you know ever needs to access them.

_____

_____

_____

_____

_____

_____

_____

_____

_____

_____

_____

_____

What are some common myths or misconceptions about stalking and harassment that you have encountered?

_____

_____

_____

_____

_____

_____

_____

_____

_____

_____

_____

_____

_____

_____

_____

_____

_____

_____

_____

_____

_____

_____

_____

_____

_____

_____

_____

_____

_____

How can you educate yourself and others to dispel these myths and better understand the reality of these behaviors?

_____

_____

_____

_____

_____

_____

_____

_____

_____

_____

_____

_____

_____

_____

_____

_____

_____

_____

_____

_____

_____

_____

_____

_____

_____

_____

_____

_____

_____

Reflect on the potential emotional and psychological effects of being a victim of stalking or harassment. What are some self-care strategies that you or others can employ to cope with the trauma of such an experience?

_____

_____

_____

_____

_____

_____

_____

_____

_____

_____

_____

_____

_____

Consider the impact that cultural norms and societal attitudes may have on the prevalence and reporting of stalking and harassment. How can we work to create a culture that takes these issues seriously and supports survivors?

_____

_____

_____

_____

_____

_____

_____

_____

_____

_____

_____

_____

_____

_____

_____

_____

_____

_____

_____

_____

_____

_____

Think about the ways in which technology has changed the landscape of stalking and harassment, particularly in the form of cyberstalking and online harassment. What steps can you take to protect your online privacy and safety, and how can we work to prevent these types of behaviors from occurring in the first place?

_____

_____

_____

_____

_____

_____

Practical tips for staying safe

Personal safety is an essential aspect of our well-being, and it's crucial to take measures to ensure it. Stalking and harassment can cause significant fear and anxiety, and it's important to be prepared with practical tips to stay safe. This chapter will provide suggestions and advice on increasing personal safety and taking preventative measures. We will also discuss the importance of self-care and seeking professional help for mental health support. By being proactive and informed, we can take steps to protect ourselves and maintain our well-being.

Suggestions for increasing personal safety, such as carrying a personal alarm or changing daily routines

❖ Carrying a personal alarm or whistle to draw attention and deter potential attackers.

❖ Avoiding walking alone at night or in areas with little visibility. If you must walk alone, consider carrying a flashlight or other source of light.

❖ Changing up your daily routine to avoid predictable patterns. For example, taking different routes to work or school, or varying the times you leave and return home.

❖ Avoiding sharing personal information, such as your home address or daily schedule, with people you don't trust.

❖ Trusting your instincts and being aware of your surroundings. If something feels off, take steps to remove yourself from the situation.

❖ Installing and using security systems, such as motion sensor lights or surveillance cameras, to monitor your home and surroundings.

❖ Taking self-defense classes or other training programs to learn how to defend yourself in dangerous situations.

❖ Staying aware of current events and local crime trends, and taking steps to protect yourself accordingly.

- ❖ Developing a safety plan with family members or trusted friends, including a plan for contacting authorities or seeking medical attention in case of emergency.

- ❖ Seeking help from local community resources, such as neighborhood watch groups or victim advocacy organizations, for additional support and guidance.

- ❖ Remember that these suggestions are not foolproof, and it's important to always trust your instincts and take steps to protect yourself in any situation.

Discussion of the importance of self-care and seeking professional help for mental health support

Self-care is an essential aspect of healing and recovery from the trauma of stalking and harassment. Survivors often struggle with feelings of anxiety, fear, and helplessness, and it can be challenging to maintain a sense of balance and well-being. However, taking steps to care for oneself can have a significant impact on mental and emotional health.

One of the most important things a survivor can do is to seek professional help. A mental health professional, such as a therapist or counselor, can provide a safe and supportive space to process emotions, work through trauma, and develop coping strategies. It can be difficult to reach out for help, but it is a crucial step in healing and recovery.

Self-care also involves taking care of one's physical health. Regular exercise, healthy eating habits, and getting enough sleep are all essential for maintaining physical and emotional well-being. Engaging in activities that bring joy and relaxation, such as hobbies or spending time with loved ones, can also be beneficial.

Another important aspect of self-care is setting boundaries and saying no when necessary. It is essential to prioritize one's own needs and limit interactions with people or situations that may be triggering or harmful.

Self-care is not selfish; it is a vital part of healing and recovery. Survivors of stalking and harassment deserve to prioritize their well-being and seek out the support and resources they need to heal and move forward.

In addition to seeking professional help and prioritizing self-care, there are practical steps that survivors can take to stay safe and prevent future instances of stalking and harassment. This includes being mindful of personal safety, such as carrying a personal alarm or changing daily routines to avoid potentially dangerous situations.

Overall, self-care is an essential part of healing and recovery for survivors of stalking and harassment. It involves taking care of oneself physically, mentally, and emotionally, and seeking professional help when necessary. Survivors deserve to prioritize their well-being and safety as they navigate the aftermath of these traumatic experiences.

Reflect on a time when you experienced harassment or stalking. How did it impact your mental health? Did you seek professional help or engage in self-care practices? If so, what were they? If not, why do you think you didn't seek help or engage in self-care?

Write about a self-care practice that helps you feel grounded and calm. Why do you think this practice works for you? How can you incorporate this practice into your daily routine?

Think about a time when you felt overwhelmed by stress or anxiety related to your experiences with harassment or stalking. What coping strategies did you use in that moment? Were they helpful or not? If not, what other strategies could you try in the future?

Write about a time when you received support from a mental health professional. What was helpful about the experience? Was there anything that didn't work for you? If you haven't sought professional help, what are some barriers that prevent you from doing so?

Reflect on your current self-care practices. Are there any practices that you'd like to add to your routine? Are there any practices that you'd like to prioritize more? Write about how you can make these changes.

Write about a time when you felt empowered in the face of harassment or stalking. What actions did you take to protect yourself? How did those actions make you feel? What can you do to continue feeling empowered in the future?

Conclusion

As survivors of stalking and harassment, it's important to understand that we are not alone. Our experiences are valid and we have the power to take action to protect ourselves and prevent future instances of these behaviors. Throughout this chapter, we have discussed the warning signs of stalking and harassment, practical tips for staying safe, and the importance of seeking professional help for mental health support.

One of the key takeaways from this chapter is the importance of recognizing warning signs early on. Unwanted communication, surveillance, and unwanted gifts or messages are just a few examples of behaviors that can indicate stalking and harassment. By being aware of these warning signs, we can take proactive steps to prevent the situation from escalating.

Another important aspect of staying safe is taking steps to protect our personal information and online presence. This includes being cautious about sharing personal information on social media and setting privacy settings to limit access to our profiles. We can also use technology to our advantage by using personal alarms or apps that can track our location.

It's also important to communicate our boundaries clearly and effectively with others. This can involve setting limits on how much personal information we share with others, being assertive when someone makes us feel uncomfortable, and seeking help from a trusted friend or authority figure if we feel unsafe.

However, it's important to recognize that taking these steps alone may not always be enough. Seeking professional help for mental health support can be crucial in processing and healing from the trauma of stalking and harassment. This can involve seeking therapy, joining a support group, or speaking with a mental health professional to develop coping strategies.

In conclusion, we have discussed the importance of recognizing warning signs, taking proactive steps to stay safe, and seeking professional help when necessary. Remember, as survivors, we have the power to take control of our situations and protect ourselves. It's important to trust our instincts, communicate effectively with others, and seek help and support when needed. We are not alone, and there is hope for healing and moving forward from these experiences.

Journal Exercises:

Reflect on the warning signs of stalking and harassment that were discussed in this book. What warning signs have you personally experienced or witnessed in others?

_____
_____
_____
_____
_____
_____
_____
_____
_____

How did you respond to those situations, and what could you have done differently?

Write about a time when you or someone you know sought help or support for stalking or harassment. What was the outcome of that situation, and how did it impact your or their well-being?

_____

_____

_____

_____

_____

_____

_____

_____

_____

_____

_____

_____

_____

_____

_____

_____

_____

_____

_____

_____

_____

_____

_____

Think about the practical tips for staying safe that were discussed in this book. Which tips do you think would be most helpful for you to implement in your daily life?

_____

_____

_____

_____

How do you think those changes could impact your sense of safety and well-being?

_____

_____

_____

_____

_____

_____

_____

_____

_____

_____

_____

_____

_____

_____

_____

_____

_____

_____

_____

_____

_____

_____

_____

_____

_____

_____

_____

Write about the importance of self-care and seeking professional help for mental health support. Have you ever struggled with mental health issues related to stalking or harassment, or do you know someone who has?

How did seeking professional help impact the situation?

Reflect on the overall message of this book - the importance of recognizing and preventing stalking and harassment. How has reading this book impacted your understanding of these issues, and what actions do you plan to take to help prevent them in the future?

_____

_____

_____

_____

Finally, write a letter to yourself reflecting on what you have learned from this book. What advice would you give to yourself moving forward, and what support or resources do you need to stay safe and healthy?

_____

_____

_____

_____

_____

_____

_____

_____

_____

_____

_____

_____

_____

_____

_____

_____

_____

_____

_____

_____

_____

_____

CHAPTER 5 COPING STRATEGIES

Strategies for managing anxiety, fear, and trauma
Coping mechanisms and self-care techniques
Tips for seeking professional help

Stalking and harassment can be incredibly traumatic experiences that leave lasting emotional scars. Coping with the fear, anxiety, and trauma that often accompany these experiences is crucial for healing and moving forward. In this chapter, we will discuss various coping strategies and self-care techniques that can help survivors manage the emotional toll of stalking and harassment. We will also explore the importance of seeking professional help and the various options available for mental health support. By learning these coping strategies, survivors can take the necessary steps to care for themselves and begin the healing process.

Strategies for managing anxiety, fear, and trauma

Dealing with the aftermath of stalking and harassment can be a traumatic experience that leaves a lasting impact on the survivor's mental health. Coping with the emotional toll of these experiences requires strategies for managing anxiety, fear, and trauma. In this chapter, we will explore various techniques that can help survivors manage the psychological effects of stalking and harassment.

One of the most important coping strategies is to develop a support network. Talking to a trusted friend, family member, or therapist can be incredibly beneficial in helping to process emotions and work through trauma. It is also important to engage in self-care activities that promote mental wellness. Exercise, meditation, and journaling are just a few examples of self-care practices that can help to reduce anxiety and improve mood.

Another important coping mechanism is to develop a sense of control over one's own life. Survivors of stalking and harassment often feel like they have lost control over their own lives and are powerless to stop the behavior of their stalker or harasser. Taking steps to regain a sense of control can be empowering and help to reduce feelings of helplessness. This can involve setting boundaries with the stalker or harasser, as well as taking legal action to protect oneself.

Cognitive behavioral therapy (CBT) is a widely recognized treatment approach that can be particularly helpful for survivors of stalking and harassment. CBT helps individuals identify and change negative thought patterns that contribute to anxiety and depression. It can also help to develop coping skills and improve overall mental health. Seeking professional help through therapy or counseling can be an important step towards healing.

Survivors can also benefit from mindfulness-based practices, such as yoga or meditation. These practices help to increase self-awareness, reduce stress, and promote relaxation. Additionally, survivors may benefit from attending support groups or participating in peer-to-peer counseling with others who have experienced stalking and harassment.

It is important to recognize that coping with the effects of stalking and harassment is a process that may take time. Healing and recovery may not happen overnight, but by developing coping strategies and seeking help when needed, survivors can take control of their lives and move forward in a positive direction.

In conclusion, managing anxiety, fear, and trauma is a critical aspect of healing from the effects of stalking and harassment. By developing coping strategies, seeking professional help, and engaging in self-care practices, survivors can take control of their lives and move forward towards a more positive future.

Journal Exercises

Reflect on a time when you felt anxious or fearful due to a past experience. What strategies did you use to manage those emotions? Did they work for you?

_____

_____

_____

_____

_____

_____

_____

_____

_____

_____

_____

_____

_____

_____

_____

_____

_____

_____

_____

_____

_____

_____

_____

_____

_____

_____

_____

If not, what could you have done differently?

_____

_____

_____

Write about a current situation that is causing you anxiety or fear. What steps can you take to manage those feelings in a healthy way?

_____

_____

_____

_____

_____

_____

_____

_____

_____

_____

_____

_____

_____

_____

_____

_____

_____

_____

_____

_____

_____

_____

Are there any coping strategies you've used in the past that could be helpful now?

_____

_____

_____

_____

_____

Identify your triggers for anxiety or fear. Is there a pattern to when and where those emotions arise? Write down some coping strategies you could use in those situations to help manage your emotions.

_____

_____

_____

_____

_____

_____

_____

_____

_____

_____

_____

_____

_____

_____

_____

_____

_____

_____

_____

_____

_____

_____

Write about a traumatic event you have experienced. How have you coped with the aftermath of that experience?

_____

_____

_____

_____

_____

_____

_____

_____

_____

Are there any strategies that have helped you to manage the emotions associated with it?

_____

_____

_____

_____

_____

_____

_____

_____

_____

_____

_____

_____

_____

_____

_____

_____

_____

_____

_____

_____

_____

_____

_____

_____

_____

_____

_____

_____

_____

Make a list of activities or hobbies that help you to relax and de-stress.
How often do you engage in these activities?

_____

_____

_____

_____

_____

_____

_____

_____

_____

_____

_____

_____

_____

_____

_____

_____

_____

_____

_____

_____

_____

_____

_____

_____

_____

_____

_____

_____

Are there any other activities you could try that might be helpful?

_____

_____

_____

_____

_____

_____

_____

_____

_____

_____

_____

_____

_____

_____

_____

_____

_____

_____

_____

_____

_____

_____

_____

_____

_____

_____

_____

_____

Write about the importance of self-care when dealing with anxiety, fear, and trauma. What are some self-care strategies you could incorporate into your daily routine?

_____

_____

_____

_____

_____

_____

_____

_____

_____

_____

_____

_____

_____

_____

_____

_____

_____

_____

How can you prioritize self-care in your life?

Coping mechanisms and self-care techniques

Of all the things that can help a survivor of stalking or harassment, coping mechanisms and self-care techniques are among the most important. Coping mechanisms are tools and strategies that help individuals manage their emotions and navigate challenging situations. Self-care, on the other hand, involves taking care of oneself physically, emotionally, and mentally. In this chapter, we will discuss various coping mechanisms and self-care techniques that can help survivors of stalking or harassment.

Establish a Support System
Having a support system is essential for anyone who has experienced stalking or harassment. A support system can include friends, family members, or professionals such as therapists or support groups. It is important to surround yourself with people who believe and support you, as well as those who can provide guidance and resources when you need them.

Practice Mindfulness
Mindfulness is the practice of being present in the moment and focusing on one's thoughts and feelings without judgment. Mindfulness

can help individuals manage anxiety, depression, and other negative emotions. Some mindfulness practices include meditation, deep breathing exercises, and yoga.

Engage in Creative Activities
Engaging in creative activities such as painting, drawing, or writing can be therapeutic for survivors of stalking or harassment. Creative activities allow individuals to express themselves in a safe and non-judgmental environment. Creative activities can also be used as a distraction from negative thoughts and emotions.

Take Care of Your Body
Taking care of your body is an essential part of self-care. This includes getting enough sleep, eating nutritious foods, and engaging in physical activity. Physical activity such as going for a walk or doing yoga can help reduce stress and improve mood.

Set Boundaries
Setting boundaries is an essential part of self-care. It is important to establish clear boundaries with family members, friends, and acquaintances. This includes saying "no" when you need to, avoiding people who make you feel uncomfortable or unsafe, and taking time for yourself when you need it.

Engage in Positive Self-Talk
Positive self-talk involves using positive affirmations and thoughts to combat negative thoughts and emotions. It is important to remember that you are not at fault for the stalking or harassment you experienced. Engaging in positive self-talk can help build self-esteem and promote a positive self-image.

Seek Professional Help
Seeking professional help is an important part of coping with stalking or harassment. A trained mental health professional can provide support and guidance as you navigate your feelings and experiences. It

is important to find a therapist who specializes in trauma and has experience working with survivors of stalking or harassment.

Take Time for Yourself

It is important to take time for yourself and engage in activities that bring you joy and relaxation. This could include taking a relaxing bath, reading a book, or watching a favorite movie. It is important to remember that taking time for yourself is not selfish but rather an essential part of self-care.

Coping mechanisms and self-care techniques are essential tools for survivors of stalking or harassment. It is important to remember that healing takes time and that everyone's healing journey is different. By engaging in self-care and coping mechanisms, survivors can begin to reclaim their lives and move forward from their experiences.

Journal Exercises

Identify your go-to self-care activities. Write a list of activities that help you feel calm, centered, and grounded. This might include things like taking a bath, going for a walk, reading a book, or meditating. Reflect on why these activities are helpful for you and how you can incorporate them into your daily routine.

_____

_____

_____

_____

_____

_____

_____

_____

_____

_____

_____

_____

_____

_____

_____

_____

_____

_____

_____

_____

_____

_____

_____

_____

_____

_____

_____

_____

_____

_____

_____

Explore new self-care practices. Brainstorm some self-care practices that you haven't tried before. This might include things like journaling, practicing yoga, or listening to guided meditations. Choose one new practice to try and write about your experience with it. Did you enjoy it?

_____

_____

_____

_____

_____

_____

_____

Did it help you feel more relaxed or centered?

_____

_____

_____

_____

_____

_____

_____

_____

_____

_____

_____

_____

_____

_____

_____

_____

_____

_____

_____

_____

_____

Write a self-care plan. Create a plan for prioritizing self-care in your daily life. Write down specific activities you will do each day to take care of yourself, such as drinking enough water, going for a walk, or taking breaks from work. Reflect on why each of these activities is important for your well-being.

_____

_____

_____

_____

_____
_____
_____
_____
_____
_____
_____
_____
_____
_____
_____
_____
_____
_____
_____
_____
_____
_____
_____
_____
_____
_____
_____
_____
_____

Reflect on your coping mechanisms. Think about how you typically cope with stress or difficult emotions. Are your coping mechanisms healthy and effective? Write about ways you can improve your coping strategies, such as by practicing mindfulness or reaching out to a trusted friend for support.

Practice gratitude. Write down three things you're grateful for each day. This can help you shift your focus away from negative thoughts and cultivate a more positive mindset.

_____

_____

_____

_____

_____

_____

_____

_____

_____

_____

_____

_____

_____

_____

_____

_____

_____

_____

_____

_____

_____

_____

_____

_____

_____

_____

_____

_____

Write a letter to yourself. Write a letter to your future self, offering words of encouragement and support. Reflect on how far you've come and the progress you've made in your healing journey.

_____

_____

_____

_____

_____

Tips for seeking professional help

➤ Research and choose a therapist or counselor who specializes in trauma or has experience working with survivors of stalking and harassment.

➤ Consider the type of therapy that may be most effective for you, such as cognitive-behavioral therapy or mindfulness-based therapy.

➤ Ask for referrals from trusted sources, such as friends, family members, or medical professionals.

➤ Be honest with your therapist about your experiences and feelings, even if they are difficult to talk about.

➤ Set realistic goals and expectations for therapy, and communicate them clearly with your therapist.

➤ Practice self-compassion and give yourself time and space to heal.

➤ Consider attending a support group for survivors of stalking or harassment, either in person or online.

➤ Seek medical attention if necessary, such as if you have physical injuries or if you are experiencing symptoms of anxiety or depression.

➤ Remember that seeking professional help is a sign of strength and courage, and that healing is a journey.

Conclusion:

In this chapter, we discussed strategies for managing anxiety, fear, and trauma, as well as coping mechanisms and self-care techniques. We also explored the importance of seeking professional help and provided tips for doing so.

It is important to remember that healing from the effects of stalking and harassment is a process that takes time and effort. Coping strategies and self-care techniques can help manage anxiety and trauma symptoms, but seeking professional help from a therapist or counselor can provide additional support and guidance.

Remember to be gentle with yourself as you navigate the healing process. Coping mechanisms and self-care techniques may take time to find what works best for you, and seeking professional help may be a daunting task, but it is a brave step towards healing.

Remember to prioritize your mental and emotional health, and never hesitate to reach out for support when needed. You deserve to feel safe and supported in your journey towards healing.

CHAPTER 6 LEGAL AND PRACTICAL CONSIDERATIONS

Understanding legal options for victims of stalking and harassment
The importance of documenting evidence
Practical advice for staying safe

Stalking and harassment are serious crimes that can have long-lasting effects on victims. In addition to the emotional toll, they can also have legal and practical consequences. It is important for victims to understand their legal options and take practical steps to protect themselves.

This chapter will provide information on the legal options available to victims of stalking and harassment, as well as practical advice for staying safe. We will also discuss the importance of documenting evidence and seeking help from professionals.

By taking these steps, victims can take control of their situation and protect themselves from further harm.

Understanding legal options for victims of stalking and harassment

Stalking and harassment are serious issues that can have significant and lasting impacts on victims. While there are a variety of coping mechanisms and self-care techniques that survivors can use to manage their trauma, it's important to also understand the legal options available for victims. In this chapter, we will discuss the various legal options that survivors have when it comes to dealing with stalking and harassment, as well as the importance of documenting evidence and seeking professional help.

One of the first steps that a survivor can take is to obtain a restraining order or protective order against their stalker or harasser. A restraining order is a court-issued document that orders an individual to stay away from the victim and refrain from contacting them in any way. A protective order, on the other hand, is a court order that requires the stalker or harasser to stop all contact with the victim, as well as other specified actions.

To obtain a restraining or protective order, a survivor must file a petition with the court. In some cases, the court may require the survivor to provide evidence of the stalking or harassment, such as threatening messages, surveillance footage, or witness testimony. Once a restraining or protective order is issued, it is important for the survivor to keep a copy of the order with them at all times and to alert law enforcement if the stalker or harasser violates the terms of the order.

Another legal option for survivors is to pursue criminal charges against their stalker or harasser. In some cases, stalking and harassment can be classified as criminal offenses, such as stalking, cyberstalking, or harassment. It is important for survivors to report any instances of stalking or harassment to law enforcement as soon as possible and to provide as much evidence as possible, such as threatening messages, phone records, or witness testimony.

Survivors may also consider pursuing civil action against their stalker or harasser. Civil action can include filing a lawsuit against the stalker or harasser for damages, such as emotional distress or lost wages. In some cases, a survivor may be able to seek a restraining order or protective order as part of the civil action.

It is important for survivors to keep a record of any evidence related to the stalking or harassment, including threatening messages, emails, social media posts, phone records, and any physical evidence such as gifts or notes. This evidence can be used in court to support the survivor's case and obtain legal protection. Additionally, survivors should keep a journal or log of all incidents related to the stalking or harassment, including dates, times, and locations.

In addition to understanding legal options, it is important for survivors to seek professional help. This can include therapy, counseling, or support groups. A mental health professional can provide survivors with coping mechanisms and self-care techniques to manage their trauma and anxiety. They can also provide survivors with guidance on documenting evidence and seeking legal help.

In conclusion, understanding legal options is an important step for survivors of stalking and harassment. Restraining and protective orders, criminal charges, and civil action are all potential legal options that survivors may consider. Additionally, survivors should document evidence and seek professional help to manage their trauma and anxiety. It is important for survivors to know that they are not alone and that there are resources available to help them through this difficult time.

The importance of documenting evidence
When it comes to dealing with stalking and harassment, documenting evidence can be crucial in protecting oneself and seeking legal action. Evidence can help establish a pattern of behavior and provide proof of the stalking or harassment, which can be difficult to prove otherwise. In this chapter, we will explore the importance of documenting evidence, what types of evidence to collect, and how to preserve it.

Firstly, it is important to understand what types of evidence can be useful in a stalking or harassment case. This can include any communication from the stalker or harasser, such as text messages, emails, social media messages, or letters. Any evidence of surveillance or tracking, such as photographs or videos, can also be useful. Additionally, evidence of any physical encounters or attacks, such as bruises or injuries, should also be documented.

One important thing to keep in mind when documenting evidence is to do so as soon as possible. Memories can fade over time, and physical evidence can be lost or destroyed. Therefore, it is important to start documenting evidence as soon as the stalking or harassment begins. This can also help establish a pattern of behavior, which can be important in proving that the behavior is ongoing and not just a one-time occurrence.

Another important aspect of documenting evidence is to be consistent in collecting it. This means keeping a record of every incident, no matter how small or insignificant it may seem. Even if it may not seem like evidence at the time, it may become important later on. This also includes keeping a record of any witnesses to the behavior.

When collecting evidence, it is important to do so in a safe and legal manner. It is important to not break any laws or put oneself in danger in the process. If collecting evidence in person, it is important to do so in a public place or with a witness present. It is also important to not tamper with any evidence or violate anyone else's privacy.

In addition to collecting evidence, it is also important to preserve it properly. This can include making copies of any communication or physical evidence, and keeping it in a safe place. It is important to not alter or edit any evidence, as this can make it inadmissible in court.

When it comes to seeking legal action, the evidence collected can be crucial in proving the case. It is important to consult with a lawyer who is experienced in stalking and harassment cases. They can help navigate the legal process and advise on the best course of action.

It is important to keep in mind that seeking legal action can be a difficult and emotional process. It is important to take care of oneself and seek support throughout the process. This can include seeking therapy or counseling, as well as relying on friends and family for emotional support.

In conclusion, documenting evidence is crucial in protecting oneself from stalking and harassment, and in seeking legal action if necessary. It is important to understand what types of evidence to collect, to be consistent in collecting it, and to preserve it properly. Seeking legal action can be a difficult process, but with the proper evidence and support, it can be a step towards healing and moving forward.

Practical advice for staying safe

When it comes to staying safe, there are several practical tips that can help prevent incidents of stalking and harassment. Here are some important things to keep in mind:

Be aware of your surroundings: One of the most effective ways to stay safe is to be aware of your surroundings at all times. This means paying attention to who is around you, staying in well-lit areas, and avoiding isolated or dangerous locations.

Trust your instincts: If something doesn't feel right, trust your instincts and take action to protect yourself. This could mean leaving the area, seeking help from others, or contacting law enforcement.

Stay connected: It's important to stay connected with friends, family, and others who can help keep you safe. Make sure someone knows where you are and who you're with, especially if you're in an unfamiliar place or situation.

Carry self-defense tools: Carrying self-defense tools like pepper spray, a personal alarm, or a small flashlight can help you protect yourself if you're ever in danger.

Change up your routine: Varying your routine and avoiding predictable patterns can make it more difficult for someone to stalk or harass you. This could mean taking a different route to work or school, changing up your gym schedule, or avoiding certain places or activities.

Use technology wisely: While technology can be helpful in many ways, it can also be a tool for stalkers and harassers. Be cautious about sharing personal information online and consider using privacy settings to limit who can see your social media profiles.

Seek support: Finally, don't hesitate to seek support from others if you're feeling threatened or unsafe. This could mean talking to a trusted friend or family member, seeking help from a counselor or therapist, or contacting a victim advocacy organization.

By following these practical tips, you can take proactive steps to protect yourself from stalking and harassment. Remember, your safety is a top priority and there are resources available to help you stay safe and seek justice if necessary.

In conclusion, navigating the legal and practical aspects of dealing with stalking and harassment can be overwhelming, but it is important to take the necessary steps to protect yourself and seek justice. Understanding your legal options and documenting evidence are critical in building a strong case, and seeking practical advice for staying safe can help prevent further incidents. Remember that you are not alone in this journey and there are resources available to support you, whether it's seeking help from a professional, contacting law enforcement, or reaching out to a support group. With the right tools and resources, you can take control of your situation and move forward towards healing and recovery.

CHAPTER 7 BUILDING RESILIENCE AND MOVING FORWARD

The importance of self-love and self-compassion
Strategies for rebuilding confidence and self-worth
Tips for developing healthy relationships and a positive outlook

Dealing with stalking or harassment can be a traumatic and emotionally draining experience, and the effects can linger long after the behavior has stopped. It can be challenging to rebuild confidence and move forward after such an experience, but it's possible with the right mindset and tools. In this chapter, we'll explore the importance of self-love and self-compassion, as well as strategies for rebuilding confidence and self-worth. Additionally, we'll discuss tips for developing healthy relationships and a positive outlook, which are essential for building resilience and moving forward from the effects of stalking and harassment. By implementing these strategies, survivors can regain their sense of self and reclaim their lives with a renewed sense of strength and purpose.

The importance of self-love and self-compassion

As a survivor of stalking and harassment, I learned that one of the most important things I needed to do was to focus on my own well-being. Self-love and self-compassion were not just buzzwords, but necessary practices for my mental and emotional health. It can be difficult to prioritize ourselves when we feel like we've been a victim, but taking care of ourselves is vital for moving forward.

Self-love means accepting and appreciating ourselves for who we are, flaws and all. It means practicing self-care and setting boundaries that honor our needs and values. Self-compassion is similar, but it involves showing ourselves kindness and understanding when we make mistakes or face challenges.

For me, learning to love and care for myself meant setting aside time for activities that made me happy and relaxed. It meant taking breaks from work and social obligations when I needed to recharge, and not feeling guilty for doing so. I also made an effort to surround myself with positive and supportive people, whether it was through therapy, support groups, or reconnecting with old friends.

But it's important to acknowledge that self-love and self-compassion are not easy. It takes time and effort to build a positive relationship with ourselves, especially after experiencing trauma. That's why it's crucial to seek professional help, such as therapy or counseling, to work through any lingering emotional pain or trauma. It's also important to remember that progress is not always linear, and setbacks are normal. Be patient and gentle with yourself on this journey.

In addition to seeking help, there are small steps we can take every day to practice self-love and self-compassion. We can start by speaking kindly to ourselves, rather than criticizing or berating ourselves for mistakes or setbacks. We can also take care of our physical health by getting enough sleep, eating nourishing foods, and engaging in regular exercise.

Ultimately, the key to building self-love and self-compassion is to make it a daily practice. It's not something we can achieve overnight, but rather something we must work on consistently. By prioritizing ourselves and our well-being, we can begin to heal from the trauma of stalking and harassment and move forward with strength and resilience.

Journal Exercises

Reflect on moments in your life when you have been hard on yourself. Write about what triggered those feelings and how you reacted to them.

Did you speak to yourself kindly, or did you engage in negative self-talk? How did that affect your mood and overall well-being?

_____

_____

_____

_____

_____

_____

_____

_____

_____

_____

_____

_____

_____

_____

_____

_____

_____

_____

_____

_____

_____

_____

_____

_____

_____

_____

_____

_____

_____

_____

_____

_____

Take some time to identify your strengths and positive qualities. Write them down and reflect on how they have helped you overcome challenges in the past. How can you use these strengths to build resilience and move forward in the future?

_____
_____
_____
_____
_____
_____
_____
_____
_____
_____
_____
_____
_____
_____
_____
_____
_____
_____
_____
_____
_____
_____
_____
_____
_____
_____
_____
_____

_____

_____

_____

Consider the messages you have received from others throughout your life about what makes someone "good" or "successful." Have these messages influenced the way you view yourself? If so, in what ways?

_____

_____

_____

_____

_____

_____

_____

_____

_____

_____

_____

_____

_____

_____

_____

_____

_____

_____

_____

_____

_____

_____

How can you challenge those messages and embrace a more compassionate and self-loving perspective?

_____

_____

_____

_____

_____

_____

Write a letter to yourself from the perspective of a kind and compassionate friend. What would they say to you to offer comfort and support? How can you internalize those messages and offer yourself the same kindness and compassion?

_____

_____

_____

_____

_____

_____

_____

_____

_____

_____

_____

_____

_____

_____

_____

_____

_____

_____

_____

_____

Think about how you currently practice self-care and self-love. What are some simple things you can do on a daily basis to prioritize your well-being and show yourself love and compassion? Write down a list of these activities and commit to incorporating them into your routine.

_____

_____

_____

_____

_____

_____

_____

_____

_____

_____

_____

_____

_____

Reflect on a recent mistake or failure. How did you react to this situation?

_____

_____

_____

_____

_____

_____

_____

_____

_____

_____

_____

_____

_____

_____

_____

_____

_____

_____

_____

_____

_____

_____

_____

_____

_____

_____

_____

_____

_____

_____

_____

_____

_____

Did you engage in self-blame or negative self-talk?

_____

_____

_____

_____

_____

_____

_____

_____

_____

_____

_____

_____

_____

_____

_____

_____

_____

_____

_____

_____

_____

_____

_____

_____

_____

_____

_____

_____

_____

_____

_____

_____

How can you reframe your thinking and offer yourself compassion and forgiveness instead? Write about how this shift in perspective can help you build resilience and move forward.

_____

_____

_____

_____

_____

_____

_____

_____

_____

_____

_____

_____

_____

_____

_____

_____

_____

_____

_____

_____

_____

_____

_____

_____

_____

_____

_____

_____

_____

_____

_____

Strategies for rebuilding confidence and self-worth

Surviving stalking or harassment can be a difficult and traumatic experience, leaving survivors feeling overwhelmed and stripped of their sense of safety and self-worth. However, it is possible to rebuild confidence and self-worth after such an experience. In this chapter, we will explore some strategies for rebuilding confidence and self-worth after experiencing stalking or harassment.

Acknowledge and Validate Your Feelings: The first step in rebuilding confidence and self-worth is to acknowledge and validate the difficult emotions that come with the experience of stalking or harassment. It is important to give yourself permission to feel these emotions, whether it be fear, anger, sadness, or guilt. By acknowledging and validating your emotions, you can begin to process them in a healthy way.

Seek Support: Survivors of stalking and harassment often feel isolated and alone. It can be helpful to seek support from friends, family, or a therapist who can provide a safe and supportive space to process your feelings and experiences. It is important to remember that seeking support is a sign of strength, not weakness.

Practice Self-Care: Taking care of yourself is crucial in rebuilding confidence and self-worth. Self-care looks different for everyone, but it can include things like getting enough sleep, eating well, engaging in physical activity, and setting aside time for relaxation and self-reflection.

Challenge Negative Self-Talk: Survivors of stalking or harassment may experience negative self-talk, such as self-blame or feelings of worthlessness. It is important to challenge these negative thoughts and replace them with positive affirmations. For example, instead of telling yourself "I am worthless," you can replace that thought with "I am strong and resilient."

Set Goals: Setting small, achievable goals can help to rebuild confidence and self-worth. These goals can be anything from making a phone call to a friend to applying for a new job. Accomplishing these goals can help to boost self-esteem and provide a sense of accomplishment.

Engage in Activities That Bring You Joy: Doing things that you enjoy can help to lift your mood and boost your confidence. This can be anything from reading a book to taking a dance class. Engaging in these activities can help to remind you of your strengths and talents.

Practice Gratitude: Focusing on gratitude can help to shift your mindset from negative to positive. Take time each day to reflect on things that you are grateful for, no matter how small. This can include things like having a supportive friend or family member, a sunny day, or a good cup of coffee.

Rebuilding confidence and self-worth after experiencing stalking or harassment takes time and effort, but it is possible. By acknowledging and validating your feelings, seeking support, practicing self-care, challenging negative self-talk, setting goals, engaging in activities that bring you joy, and practicing gratitude, you can begin to rebuild your confidence and self-worth. Remember to be patient and kind to yourself throughout this process.

Journal Exercises

Write about a time when you felt confident and proud of yourself. What were you doing? How did you feel? What qualities or strengths did you demonstrate in that moment?

_____

_____

_____

_____

_____

_____

_____

_____

_____

_____

_____

_____

_____

_____

_____

_____

_____

_____

_____

_____

_____

_____

_____

_____

_____

_____

_____

_____

_____

_____

_____

_____

Make a list of things that make you feel good about yourself. Include anything from accomplishments, to physical sensations, to positive feedback from others. Reflect on why each item on the list is important to you.

_____

_____

_____

_____

_____

_____

_____

_____

_____

_____

_____

_____

_____

_____

_____

_____

_____

_____

_____

_____

_____

_____

_____

_____

_____

_____

_____

_____

Write about a time when you felt like you failed or fell short of your own expectations. What emotions did you experience? How did you respond to those feelings? What can you learn from that experience to help you build resilience and self-compassion?

_____

_____

_____

_____

_____

_____

_____

_____

_____

_____

_____

_____

_____

_____

_____

_____

_____

_____

_____

_____

_____

_____

_____

_____

_____

_____

_____

_____

_____

Reflect on the negative self-talk that you use about yourself. What kinds of things do you say to yourself? Are they true? How do they make you feel? Write down an alternative, more positive thought or affirmation to replace each negative thought.

_____

_____

_____

_____

_____

_____

_____

_____

_____

_____

_____

_____

_____

_____

_____
_____
_____
_____
_____
_____
_____
_____
_____
_____
_____
_____
_____
_____
_____
_____
_____
_____

Think of a role model or mentor who embodies qualities that you admire or would like to develop in yourself. What are those qualities? How can you work to cultivate those qualities in your own life? Write a letter to your future self, celebrating your progress in building confidence and self-worth. Include specific accomplishments or milestones that you hope to achieve, and express confidence and belief in yourself.

Tips for developing healthy relationships and a positive outlook

As a survivor of stalking and harassment, I know how challenging it can be to trust others and build healthy relationships. The trauma of such experiences can leave us feeling isolated, vulnerable, and disconnected from the world around us. But I also know that it's possible to move forward and create a fulfilling life after such trauma.

In this chapter, I'll share some tips and strategies that have helped me develop healthy relationships and maintain a positive outlook.

Start with Self-Awareness
Before we can build healthy relationships with others, we need to understand our own needs, values, and boundaries. Take some time to reflect on your past experiences, and consider what you need in a relationship to feel safe, respected, and valued. This might involve setting boundaries around communication or physical contact, or being more assertive about your needs and preferences.

Surround Yourself with Supportive People
Having a strong support system is essential for healing from trauma and building healthy relationships. This might include friends, family members, or a therapist who can offer emotional support, encouragement, and practical advice. Seek out people who are empathetic, non-judgmental, and able to listen without trying to fix or solve your problems.

Take Time to Heal
Recovering from trauma takes time and patience. It's important to give yourself permission to grieve, process your emotions, and take care of your mental and physical health. This might involve seeking professional help, such as therapy or counseling, or engaging in self-care activities like meditation, exercise, or creative expression.

Practice Communication Skills
Effective communication is essential for building healthy relationships. Practice expressing your thoughts and feelings in a clear and respectful way, and listen actively to others without interrupting or making assumptions. Seek out opportunities to practice communication skills in low-stakes settings, such as with a friend or family member, and gradually build up to more challenging situations.

Focus on Shared Values and Interests
Healthy relationships are built on mutual respect, trust, and shared values and interests. Look for people who share your passions and hobbies, or who are committed to causes or activities that are important to you. This can help create a sense of connection and purpose, and give you a shared sense of identity.

Be Patient and Forgiving
Building healthy relationships takes time and effort, and there may be setbacks or misunderstandings along the way. Practice patience and forgiveness with yourself and others, and be willing to work through challenges together. Remember that no one is perfect, and that healthy relationships are built on a foundation of trust, respect, and empathy.

Celebrate Your Progress
As you work towards building healthy relationships, take time to celebrate your progress and acknowledge your achievements. This might involve setting goals and tracking your progress, or reflecting on positive experiences and relationships that have brought joy and meaning to your life. Celebrating your progress can help build confidence and a sense of self-worth, and keep you motivated to continue moving forward.

Building healthy relationships after experiencing stalking and harassment can be a difficult and daunting process, but it's also essential for healing and moving forward. By focusing on self-awareness, communication skills, shared values, and a positive outlook, we can create fulfilling relationships that bring joy, connection, and meaning to our lives. Remember to be patient and compassionate with yourself along the way, and to seek out the support and resources you need to build a strong foundation for the future.

Journal Exercises

Gratitude journaling: Write down three things you are grateful for each day. Focus on positive aspects of your life and relationships.

_____
_____
_____
_____
_____
_____
_____
_____
_____
_____
_____
_____
_____
_____
_____
_____
_____
_____
_____
_____
_____
_____
_____
_____
_____
_____
_____
_____
_____
_____
_____
_____
_____
_____
_____

Reflect on past relationships: Think about what worked and what didn't work in your past relationships. Write about what you learned from these experiences and how you can apply that knowledge to future relationships.

_____

_____

_____

_____

_____

_____

_____

Set healthy boundaries: Write about the boundaries you want to set in your relationships. What are your deal-breakers? What are the things you're willing to compromise on?

_____

_____

_____

_____

_____

_____

_____

_____

_____

_____

_____

_____

_____

_____

_____

_____

_____

_____

_____

_____

Identify toxic patterns: Write about any toxic patterns you've noticed in your past or current relationships. How can you recognize these patterns in the future and avoid them?

_____

_____

_____

_____

_____

_____

_____

_____

_____

_____

_____

_____

Affirmations: Write positive affirmations about yourself and your relationships. Repeat these affirmations to yourself daily to help shift your mindset to a more positive outlook.

_____

_____

_____

_____

_____

_____

_____

_____

_____

_____

_____

_____

_____

_____

_____

_____

_____

Self-reflection: Reflect on your own behavior in your relationships. Write about any patterns you've noticed and how you can work on improving those behaviors.

Communication skills: Write about ways you can improve your communication skills in your relationships. Practice active listening and expressing your thoughts and feelings in a clear and respectful manner.

Forgiveness: Write about any grudges or resentments you're holding onto in your relationships. Work on forgiveness and letting go of past hurts to move forward in a positive way.

_____

_____

_____

_____

_____

_____

_____

_____

_____

_____

_____

_____

_____

_____

_____

_____

_____

_____

_____

_____

_____

_____

_____

Celebrate the positives: Write about the positive qualities in your relationships and the things you appreciate about your loved ones. Celebrate these positives and focus on them instead of dwelling on the negatives.

_____

_____

_____

_____

_____

_____

_____

_____

_____

_____

_____

_____

_____

_____

_____

_____

_____

_____

_____

_____

_____

_____

_____

_____

_____

_____

_____

_____

_____

_____

_____

Take action: Write down specific actions you can take to improve your relationships and develop a more positive outlook. Make a plan and commit to implementing these changes in your life.

_____

_____

In conclusion, building resilience and moving forward after experiencing stalking and harassment is a difficult journey, but it is possible. It requires a combination of self-love, self-compassion, and practical strategies for rebuilding confidence and developing healthy relationships. Remember to be patient with yourself and celebrate even the small victories along the way.

It's important to continue practicing self-care and seeking professional help when necessary. Keep in mind that everyone's healing journey is unique, and what works for one person may not work for another. Be open to trying new strategies and finding what works best for you.

Above all, remember that you are not alone in this experience, and it is not your fault. You deserve to live a life free from fear and anxiety, and by taking the necessary steps to build resilience and move forward, you can achieve that goal. Keep pushing forward, and don't be afraid to ask for help when you need it.

CHAPTER 8 UPLIFTING QUOTES

Chapter 8 is a collection of inspiring and uplifting quotes from survivors of stalking and harassment, as well as thought leaders and advocates. These quotes are intended to provide comfort, support, and encouragement to those who have experienced or are currently experiencing these traumas. It can be difficult to find the words to express the complex emotions and experiences that come with being a survivor, but these quotes offer powerful insights and reminders that you are not alone and that healing and recovery are possible. Whether you are in the midst of a difficult journey or simply seeking some inspiration, these quotes can serve as a beacon of hope and a reminder of your strength and resilience.

Inspiring and uplifting quotes from survivors and thought leaders

❖ "You have been assigned this mountain to show others it can be moved." - Mel Robbins

❖ "The greatest glory in living lies not in never falling, but in rising every time we fall." - Nelson Mandela

❖ "The only way to do great work is to love what you do." - Steve Jobs

❖ "The only limit to our realization of tomorrow will be our doubts of today." - Franklin D. Roosevelt

❖ "I can be changed by what happens to me. But I refuse to be reduced by it." - Maya Angelou

❖ "The moment you give up is the moment you let someone else win." - Kobe Bryant

- ❖ "Success is not final, failure is not fatal: it is the courage to continue that counts." - Winston Churchill

- ❖ "Believe you can and you're halfway there." - Theodore Roosevelt

- ❖ "The best way to predict the future is to create it." - Abraham Lincoln

- ❖ "When you have a dream, you've got to grab it and never let go." - Carol Burnett

- ❖ "Difficult roads often lead to beautiful destinations." - Zig Ziglar

- ❖ "You are never too old to set another goal or to dream a new dream." - C.S. Lewis

- ❖ "The most common way people give up their power is by thinking they don't have any." - Alice Walker

- ❖ "If you want to go fast, go alone. If you want to go far, go together." - African proverb

- ❖ "You may encounter many defeats, but you must not be defeated." - Maya Angelou

- ❖ "The only person you are destined to become is the person you decide to be." - Ralph Waldo Emerson

- ❖ "Success is liking yourself, liking what you do, and liking how you do it." - Maya Angelou

- ❖ "Believe in yourself and all that you are. Know that there is something inside you that is greater than any obstacle." - Christian D. Larson

- ❖ "We may encounter many defeats but we must not be defeated." - Maya Angelou

- ❖ "The way to get started is to quit talking and begin doing." - Walt Disney

- ❖ "The most beautiful people we have known are those who have known defeat, known suffering, known struggle, known loss, and have found their way out of the depths." - Elizabeth Kubler-Ross

- ❖ "Life isn't about waiting for the storm to pass, it's about learning how to dance in the rain." - Vivian Greene

- ❖ "Courage doesn't always roar. Sometimes courage is the quiet voice at the end of the day saying, 'I will try again tomorrow.'" - Mary Anne Radmacher

- ❖ "The secret of change is to focus all of your energy, not on fighting the old, but on building the new." - Socrates

- ❖ "You can't fall if you don't climb. But there's no joy in living your whole life on the ground." - Unknown

- ❖ "When one door of happiness closes, another opens, but often we look so long at the closed door that we do not see the one that has been opened for us." - Helen Keller

- ❖ "Our greatest glory is not in never falling, but in rising every time we fall." - Confucius

- ❖ "Happiness can be found even in the darkest of times, if one only remembers to turn on the light." - Albus Dumbledore

- ❖ "The only true wisdom is in knowing you know nothing." - Socrates

- ❖ "You have within you right now, everything you need to deal with whatever the world can throw at you." - Brian Tracy

- ❖ "The only way to do great work is to love what you do." - Steve Jobs

- ❖ "Never let your past dictate who you are, but let it be a lesson that strengthens the person you will become." - Unkown

- ❖ "You are not a victim. No matter what you have been through, you're still here. You may have been challenged, hurt, betrayed, beaten, and discouraged, but nothing has defeated you. You are still here! You have been delayed but not denied. You are not a victim, you are a victor. You have a history of victory." - Steve Maraboli

- ❖ "Life isn't about waiting for the storm to pass... It's about learning to dance in the rain." - Vivian Greene

- ❖ "Happiness is not something ready-made. It comes from your own actions." - Dalai Lama XIV

- ❖ "You can't go back and change the beginning, but you can start where you are and change the ending." - C.S. Lewis

- ❖ "Believe in yourself, take on your challenges, dig deep within yourself to conquer fears. Never let anyone bring you down. You got this." - Chantal Sutherland

- ❖ "You may not control all the events that happen to you, but you can decide not to be reduced by them." - Maya Angelou

- ❖ "The future belongs to those who believe in the beauty of their dreams." - Eleanor Roosevelt

- ❖ "If you want to go fast, go alone. If you want to go far, go together." - African Proverb

- ❖ "We may encounter many defeats, but we must not be defeated." - Maya Angelou

- ❖ "The best way to predict your future is to create it." - Abraham Lincoln

- ❖ "The only limit to our realization of tomorrow will be our doubts of today." - Franklin D. Roosevelt

- ❖ "You are never too old to set another goal or to dream a new dream." - C.S. Lewis

- ❖ "It is during our darkest moments that we must focus to see the light." - Aristotle

- ❖ "It's not what happens to you, but how you react to it that matters." - Epictetus

- ❖ "Strength does not come from winning. Your struggles develop your strengths. When you go through hardships and decide not to surrender, that is strength." - Arnold Schwarzenegger

- ❖ "You are capable of more than you know. Choose a goal that seems right for you and strive to be the best, however hard the path. Aim high. Behave honorably. Prepare to be alone at times, and to endure failure. Persist! The world needs all you can give." - E.O. Wilson

- ❖ "In the end, we will remember not the words of our enemies, but the silence of our friends." - Martin Luther King Jr.

- ❖ "Don't let yesterday take up too much of today." - Will Rogers

CHAPTER 9 CONCLUSION

Final thoughts and words of encouragement
Recap of the key takeaways from the book

As we come to the end of this book, it's important to reflect on the valuable information and insights that have been shared throughout. We've discussed the many challenges that survivors of stalking and harassment face, from fear and anxiety to legal and practical considerations. We've explored coping strategies, self-care techniques, and the importance of seeking help from professionals. We've also touched on the importance of self-love, resilience, and positive relationships.

In this final chapter, we'll wrap up with some final thoughts and words of encouragement for anyone who may be struggling with the effects of stalking and harassment. We'll also recap the key takeaways from this book, so that you can have a clear understanding of the important lessons and strategies that you can use to move forward.
Final thoughts and words of encouragement

As I sit here reflecting on my journey as a survivor of stalking and harassment, I am filled with a mix of emotions. There were times when I felt completely alone and helpless, unsure if I would ever be able to escape the grip of my abuser. But now, looking back, I see that I have come so far. I have found my strength, my voice, and my power.

If you are reading this, you may be in the midst of your own journey. You may be feeling scared, overwhelmed, and alone. But please know that you are not alone. There is a community of survivors who have been through similar experiences and who are here to support you.

The road ahead may not be easy, but I want to remind you that you are strong, resilient, and capable of overcoming anything. You have already taken the first step by acknowledging what is happening to you and seeking help. You have the power to take control of your life and move forward.

As you continue on your journey, I encourage you to prioritize self-care and surround yourself with positive and supportive people. Seek out therapy or counseling if you need it, and don't be afraid to reach out to advocacy organizations or law enforcement for help.

Remember that healing is a process and it may take time, but it is possible. You deserve to live a life free from fear and abuse. You deserve to be happy and to feel safe.

I also want to remind you that none of this was your fault. You did not deserve to be stalked or harassed, and you are not responsible for your abuser's actions. It's okay to feel angry, sad, or frustrated, but please don't blame yourself.

In conclusion, I want to express my gratitude to those who have supported me on my journey and to those who have shared their own stories. We are stronger together and by speaking out and supporting one another, we can create a world where stalking and harassment are not tolerated.

I believe in you and I am proud of you. Keep moving forward and never give up hope.

Recap of the key takeaways from the book

As I come to the end of this book, I can't help but feel both relieved and proud. Relieved to have shared my story and proud of the progress I've made in my healing journey. I hope that my experiences and insights have provided valuable guidance for those who may be struggling with stalking and harassment.

Throughout this book, I have touched on a range of topics, from understanding the warning signs and the importance of documenting evidence to seeking professional help and developing coping mechanisms. But at the heart of it all is one message: you are not alone, and you are not to blame.

Stalking and harassment can be isolating and can make you feel like you are at fault for what is happening to you. But that couldn't be further from the truth. It's essential to remember that the behavior of the stalker or harasser is not your fault, and there is no excuse for their actions. It's also important to recognize that seeking help and support is not a sign of weakness but rather a show of strength.

One of the key takeaways from this book is the importance of recognizing the warning signs of stalking and harassment. By understanding these signs, you can take proactive steps to prevent escalation and protect yourself from harm. It's also important to document any evidence of the stalking or harassment, whether it's through saving messages, keeping a log of incidents, or obtaining a restraining order.

Seeking professional help is another critical step in the healing process. A therapist or counselor can provide a safe and supportive space for you to process your experiences and develop coping mechanisms for managing anxiety, fear, and trauma. It's also important to prioritize self-care and to take steps to rebuild your confidence and self-worth.

Building a support system of trusted friends, family members, or support groups can also be incredibly helpful. You don't have to go through this alone, and having a network of people who understand what you're going through can make all the difference.

Finally, it's essential to remember that healing is not a linear process, and it's okay to have setbacks along the way. The most important thing is to continue to show yourself love and compassion and to keep moving forward, one step at a time.

In conclusion, I want to reiterate that you are not alone, and there is hope for healing and recovery. Remember to trust your instincts, document any evidence, seek professional help, prioritize self-care, and build a support system. With time, patience, and persistence, you can reclaim your power and move forward with confidence and strength.

CHAPTER 10 EPILOGUE

Additional resources and support for those affected by stalking and
harassment
Information on organizations and support groups

While this book has provided a comprehensive guide to dealing with
stalking and harassment, it is important to recognize that recovery is an
ongoing process. It can be helpful to seek out additional resources and
support as needed. This chapter provides information on organizations
and support groups that can provide additional assistance and guidance
for those affected by stalking and harassment. Remember that you are
not alone, and there is help available to you.

**Additional resources and support for those affected by stalking and
harassment**

If you or someone you know is being stalked or harassed, it is
important to know that there are resources available to help. This
chapter will provide an overview of some of the resources and support
options that are available.

National Domestic Violence Hotline: The National Domestic Violence
Hotline is a 24/7 confidential hotline that provides support, resources,
and referrals to individuals affected by domestic violence, including
stalking and harassment. The hotline can be reached at 1-800-799-7233
or via online chat.

National Stalking Resource Center: The National Stalking Resource
Center is a program of the National Center for Victims of Crime that
provides information and resources on stalking to victims, service
providers, and the public. Their website offers information on safety
planning, legal issues, and support services, as well as a directory of
local victim service providers.

Rape, Abuse & Incest National Network (RAINN): RAINN is the nation's largest anti-sexual violence organization and offers a 24/7 confidential hotline (1-800-656-HOPE) that provides support, information, and referrals to individuals affected by sexual violence, including stalking.

VictimConnect Resource Center: VictimConnect is a program of the National Center for Victims of Crime that provides referrals and resources to victims of all types of crime, including stalking and harassment. The resource center can be reached at 1-855-4VICTIM or via online chat.

Legal Aid: Many cities and states have legal aid organizations that provide free or low-cost legal assistance to individuals who cannot afford an attorney. These organizations can provide assistance with obtaining restraining orders, navigating the legal system, and other legal issues related to stalking and harassment.

Support Groups: Support groups can be a valuable resource for individuals affected by stalking and harassment. Many organizations, such as the National Stalking Resource Center, offer online and in-person support groups for victims.

Therapy and Counseling: Seeking therapy or counseling can be helpful for individuals who have experienced stalking and harassment. A mental health professional can provide support, coping strategies, and tools for managing symptoms of trauma and anxiety.

Workplace Support: If you are being stalked or harassed in the workplace, it is important to reach out to your employer's human resources department or employee assistance program for support and guidance.

Law Enforcement: If you feel that you are in immediate danger, contact law enforcement right away. Document any incidents of stalking or harassment, including dates, times, and details of what happened, to provide to law enforcement.

It is important to remember that there is no one-size-fits-all solution to dealing with stalking and harassment. What works for one person may not work for another. It is important to reach out for help and support and to take steps to prioritize your safety and well-being.

Information on organizations and support groups

When facing stalking and harassment, it is important to remember that you are not alone. There are numerous organizations and support groups available to provide resources, guidance, and a sense of community to individuals who have experienced stalking and harassment.

National Domestic Violence Hotline:
The National Domestic Violence Hotline provides confidential support and assistance to victims and survivors of domestic violence, including stalking. The hotline operates 24/7 and provides resources for safety planning, legal support, and counseling. You can call the hotline at 1-800-799-7233 or chat with a representative online at www.thehotline.org.

Stalking Resource Center:
The Stalking Resource Center is a program of the National Center for Victims of Crime and provides a variety of resources and support to individuals who have experienced stalking, including online educational resources, referrals to local services, and training and technical assistance to professionals working with victims. Visit their website at www.stalkingawareness.org to learn more.

National Center for Victims of Crime:
The National Center for Victims of Crime provides resources and support to individuals who have experienced a variety of crimes, including stalking and harassment. They offer a helpline at 1-855-484-

2846 and have a directory of victim services available on their website at www.victimsofcrime.org.

RAINN (Rape, Abuse & Incest National Network):
RAINN is the nation's largest anti-sexual violence organization and provides resources and support to individuals affected by sexual violence, including stalking. They operate a hotline at 1-800-656-4673 and offer online chat support at www.rainn.org.

Loveisrespect:
Loveisrespect provides resources and support to individuals affected by dating violence, including stalking. They operate a helpline at 1-866-331-9474 and offer online chat support at www.loveisrespect.org.

National Network to End Domestic Violence (NNEDV):
NNEDV is a social change organization dedicated to creating a culture where domestic violence is not tolerated. They provide resources and support to individuals affected by domestic violence, including stalking. Their website at www.nnedv.org includes a directory of local domestic violence organizations and information about domestic violence laws.

VictimConnect:
VictimConnect provides resources and support to individuals affected by all types of crime, including stalking. They operate a helpline at 1-855-4VICTIM and offer online chat support at www.victimconnect.org.

National Organization for Victim Assistance (NOVA):
NOVA provides resources and support to individuals affected by all types of crime, including stalking. They offer a helpline at 1-800-TRY-NOVA and have a directory of victim services available on their website at www.trynova.org.

SurvJustice:
SurvJustice provides legal advocacy and support to survivors of sexual violence, including stalking. Their services include assistance with civil

litigation and Title IX complaints, as well as training and education for professionals. Visit their website at www.survjustice.org to learn more.

Women's Law:
Women's Law provides legal information and resources to individuals affected by domestic violence, including stalking. Their website at www.womenslaw.org includes state-specific legal information and a directory of local legal services.

These organizations and support groups are just a few of the many resources available to individuals affected by stalking and harassment. It is important to reach out for support and utilize the resources available to you. Remember, you are not alone and there is help and support available

www.ingramcontent.com/pod-product-compliance
Lightning Source LLC
Chambersburg PA
CBHW051305120626
46547CB00015B/2097